# GERRY, GET YOUR GUN

Caitlin Press Inc.
8100 Alderwood Road,
Halfmoon Bay, BC V0N 1Y1
www.caitlin-press.com

Cover and text design by Vici Johnstone
A special thanks to Michael Calvert for his help with the back cover
copy.

Printed in Canada

Caitlin Press Inc. acknowledges financial support from the Government
of Canada through the Canada Book Fund and the Canada Council for
the Arts, and from the Province of British Columbia through the British
Columbia Arts Council and the Book Publisher's Tax Credit.

Library and Archives Canada Cataloguing in Publication

Bracewell, Gerry, author
    Gerry, get your gun : my life as a hunting guide and
other adventures / Gerry Bracewell.

ISBN 978-1-927575-71-0 (pbk.)

    1. Bracewell, Gerry.  2. Women hunting guides—British
Columbia—Chilcotin Forest—Biography.  3. Women hunters—
British Columbia—Chilcotin Forest—Biography.  I. Title.

SK17.B73A3 2015          799.292'52          C2015-900550-7

# GERRY, GET YOUR GUN

## My Life as a Hunting Guide
## and Other Adventures

### BC's First Woman to Become
### a Licensed Hunting Guide

# GERRY BRACEWELL

## CAITLIN PRESS

# CONTENTS

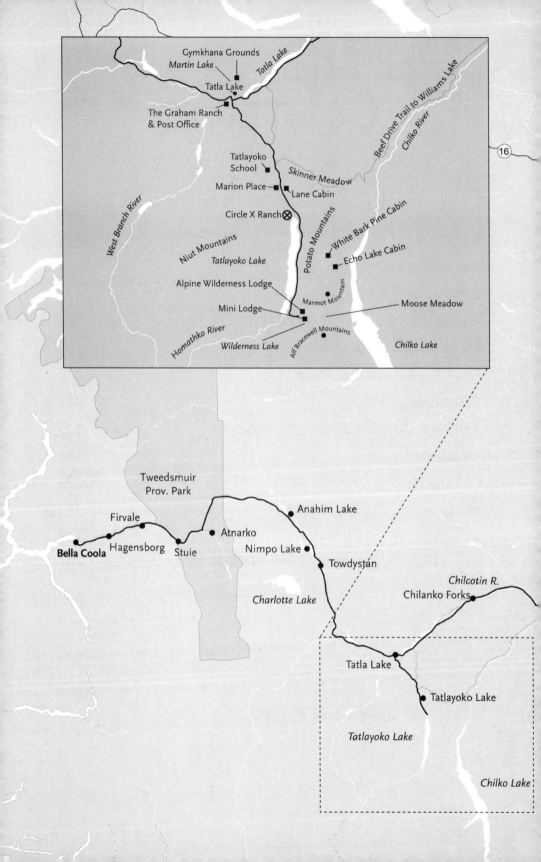

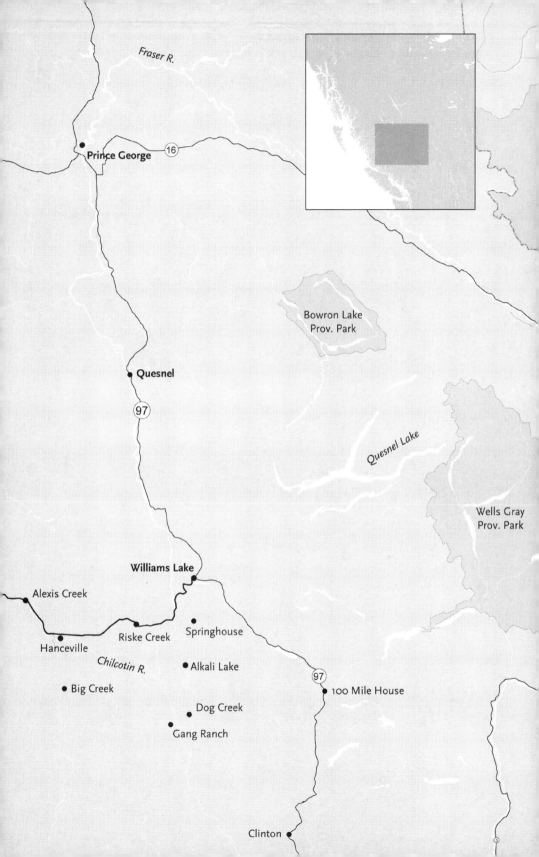

# FOREWORD

by Sage Birchwater

It is hard to imagine a better ambassador for the Chilcotin than Gerry Bracewell.

When she was four years old, growing up on the prairies near Edmonton, Gerry told her mother she wanted to live in the mountains. Her dream came true when she was sixteen years old. In the fall of 1938, Ethel Lovell, as she was known then, jumped on a train with her older sister, Mabel, bound for Vancouver. Her excitement mounted as they approached the foothills of the Rockies because she wanted to see the mountains up close. Unfortunately darkness descended before they got there, and she had to bide her time as the train wound its way through British Columbia during the night.

Come morning, she was greeted by the spectacular backdrop of Vancouver's North Shore mountains. It was everything she might have imagined, except that life in the city was a bit too crowded for this young woman used to wide-open spaces.

Ethel got a job as a governess and housekeeper for the winter. While pushing the baby carriage with her charge down the street one day, she met another young nanny by the name of Elsa, also wheeling a child in a pram. They became fast friends and decided to go to a dance together.

While riding in a streetcar on the way to the dance in Vancouver's Moose Hall, they had an epiphany. The two women decided to create new identities for themselves. Elsa adopted the name Jacquie, and Ethel decided to call herself Gerry. She has stuck with that name ever since.

As the winter wore on, Gerry told her younger brother, Robert, that she pined for a job on a ranch. While he was wheeling about the province on his motorcycle, Robert met Big Creek rancher Dick Church, who was looking for domestic help for the summer. Gerry jumped at the opportunity.

Big Creek was beautiful ranching country on the high Chilcotin Plateau west of Williams Lake. Vistas of the Coast Range could be seen in the distance. Then one day Dick Church's niece, Isobel (Issy) Moore, stopped overnight with a string of horses she was bringing from her father's place in Tatlayoko Valley to her mother's place in Bralorne.

During this brief encounter, the two young women became friends. Gerry was intrigued by Issy's description of Tatlayoko Valley surrounded on all sides by mountains. When Issy stopped by again on her way back to Tatlayoko, she encouraged Gerry to write to her father, KB Moore, to see if he might hire her the following year.

Gerry spent one more winter as a governess in Vancouver and was thrilled when KB Moore answered her letter and offered her a job as a companion to Issy on his Circle X cattle ranch. When she arrived in Tatlayoko Valley in the spring of 1940, after taking the train from Squamish to Williams Lake and catching a ride with mail-truck driver, Tommy Hodgson, across the Chilcotin Plateau, Gerry knew she was home.

She spent two years chasing horses and cattle and learning the ways of the country with Issy. They went trapping, hunting and building log cabins together. Then Issy married Ben Wilson, and life as they knew it changed. Issy and Ben got their own place further up the valley, and Gerry stayed on to work for KB Moore, who had become the father figure she never knew as a child.

In the spring of 1943, Gerry married KB's only son, Beverly Moore, and in short order they had two sons, Marty and Barry. The marriage was short-lived, and Bev left after three or four years.

Mountains and the wilds of the West Chilcotin became Gerry's lifeblood as she ranged the Circle X cattle in the alpine and went on beef drives to Williams Lake. Under KB's direction, she learned to guide big-game hunters in the high country. After apprenticing for three years, Gerry became British Columbia's first registered female big-game guide, licensed to take hunters into the wild.

Gerry has always courted destiny.

In September 1953, she knew the brand new road through the Coast Mountains from Bella Coola to the Chilcotin Plateau was nearing completion. KB Moore had given her a windup movie camera for her thirty-first birthday, and Gerry figured there should be a public record of this historic event.

With a competent hay crew back home putting up the winter forage at the Circle X Ranch, Gerry seized the moment to load her two young sons, Marty, nine, and Barry, eight, into her pickup truck and drive to the end of the road at Anahim Lake. There she rented some horses to take them to the construction site on the Bella Coola Hill where two bulldozers, coming from opposite directions, were due to meet.

Gerry got some film footage of the two bulldozers, but she had to return home to her hay crew two weeks before the road would be completed. She entrusted her camera to Alf Bracewell, one of the two Cat operators, and he made sure that the historic moment of the meeting of the Cats was captured. Six months later, Gerry and Alf Bracewell were married.

Somewhere along the way Gerry figured out that the pristine backcountry of the Chilcotin and her mountain paradise had a value worth sharing with others. It started with big-game hunters coming back year after year whether they got any animals or not. The adventure alone was worth the money they paid. Soon Gerry started leading "soft adventure" tours, where animals were not hunted and trail riders accompanied her on horseback into the alpine.

Gerry has always been a tenacious supporter of the Chilcotin: lobbying for a new school in Tatlayoko Valley, fighting for better roads, demanding improvements to the postal service and standing up for tourism. When the Cariboo Tourist Association (CTA) formed in the 1960s, Gerry became the first director representing the Chilcotin. She spent a lifetime promoting the land west of the Fraser River as a place worth visiting and saw its world-class potential as unique and special.

Gerry's dedication to tourism hasn't gone unnoticed. Bill Van Es, chair of the West Chilcotin Tourism Association and owner of Escott Bay Resort in Anahim Lake, says Gerry's hard work ensured that the word "Chilcotin" means a true wilderness area in which the pioneer spirit can still flourish in this unspoiled and timeless part of British Columbia.

"In a world where guide outfitting was mostly a male-dominated business, she carved her place as a passionate individual who could hold her own in any situation," Bill says. "Thank you, Gerry!"

Pat Corbett (chair of the Cariboo Chilcotin Coast Tourism Association and president/owner of the Hills Health Ranch & Spa in 108 Mile House) says Gerry is a pioneer in every sense of the word: "Her stories of survival in the west are right out of the movies. The hardships she endured, the many encounters with wildlife and nature itself would frighten the most hardened of outdoor enthusiasts of today. Through it all, she remains one of the finest ladies in the land. A finer lady you will not find! Her stories in this book are but a very small glimpse of a life, of true western adventure in BC's remotest cattle country."

At ninety-three years old, Gerry continues to hold court at Bracewell's Alpine Wilderness Resort, which her husband and sons started building nearly forty years ago at the foot of the Potato Mountains. Her youngest son, Alex Bracewell, runs the wilderness tourism business there now, with help from his children, Bobi, Aaron and Anna.

Though Gerry no longer heads out on horseback, she relishes the stories of the trail brought back to her by guests and family members. She is still very much part of the Alpine Wilderness experience as she adds her own tales and insights from her seventy-five years in the country. Her presence in the great lodge her family carved by hand adds ambiance that money can't buy. Gerry and her family welcome visitors. For information about the lodge visit www. bracewell.com.

# THE EARLY DAYS

I was born in 1922 at the stump farm my parents owned in Halfway Lake, Alberta, about fifty miles northwest of Edmonton. My mother had a midwife who came to settlers' homesteads to deliver their babies, and Mom must have been happy with her because she named me after her in appreciation.

My mother had a Scottish and Irish background and was eighteen when she met my dad, who had just emigrated from England. They married and had seven children, but only four of us survived.

Sadly, when I was young my father went on a fishing trip up north, and when he came back he had contracted spinal meningitis. After that he was confined to his bed and died soon after. This left my mother with all four children to raise on her own. By then my brother Leonard was twelve, my sister Mabel was ten, I was five and our little brother, Robert, was three.

Times were very hard for a young mother, and she felt so burdened trying to run the household without her husband that she "loaned" Leonard to an elderly bachelor who needed the help of a young, spirited lad in exchange for food and lodging. Mabel was enrolled into a girls' Christian school on the outskirts of Calgary where she had to work to pay for her tuition as well as her room and board.

That left us two youngsters, Bob and me, at home. Mom received a monthly government cheque of five dollars, called the "Mothers' allowance," which, in 1927, seemed like a lot of cash.

To keep us all housed and fed, my tiny five-foot mother worked

Even when I was young I loved to care for animals.

My mother and father on their wedding day.

When my father died, my mother was left with four young children.

on farms that needed help milking cows and making butter and bread, or working in the garden. Mom was a good worker, as well as a cheerful person, despite her difficulties. She had a great voice and she would sing and dance the singular dance, clog or Riverdance, while she went about her duties. She would never sing in public, though. She was far too shy.

Mom also thought of a way of making a little extra cash: the farms where she worked raised wheat, which was threshed but needed cleaning. If the farm had a cleaning mill (fanning mill) that separated the grain from the chaff, she knew that this chaff could feed chickens. Mom bought unsexed chicks to raise, fed them the chaff and then sold her eggs for two cents a dozen to the stores in our small country town. We ate the roosters, so it worked out well.

Mom always worked on farms that were within walking distance to a school. Classes only went to grade eight, but Mom was determined that Bob and I got an education. Once we got to high school we would walk five miles to town, or some winters we would move to town so we were closer.

At five years old I tamed a young calf as a pet and eventually began riding it as it grew bigger. The farm we lived on had a gentle team of Percheron mares named Queenie and Dolly. They were black and medium-sized, and they became my good friends. I used to go to visit them in their stalls in the barn. I would climb up the rails that separated them and crawl over onto Dolly's broad back and stretch out, my head pillowed on her rump and my legs dangling beside both sides of her ribcage. She was so warm, and I would lie there and daydream while she munched her hay until my mom called me to supper.

When the mares were pastured, resting in what we called the "back forty," and they needed to be brought in to work, I would ride my calf, whom I had named Skeezics, out to fetch them. When we got to the horses Dolly would lower her head to let me put on her halter. Then I would lead her to a rock or stump so I could climb onto her back. I would ride Dolly back and head for the barnyard with Queenie and my calf following. This was my chore, and I was so proud to do it.

When my little brother, Bob, was six and was old enough to attend school, we would ride Dolly through the deep snow for three miles, even in cold winter weather. We rode her bareback, which helped keep us warm. There was a barn at the school, and hay for the horses.

One neighbour had a box sleigh and team for his kids, so sometimes he would pick us up. We would crawl in to sit on the built-in benches and stay warm, sheltered from the wind. The box had a window and a slit for the reins to come through. There was only one door, and it was on the driver's side. That was the only box sleigh I ever saw.

There was always a lot of wind on that semi-prairie area of Alberta. It drifted snow over the tumbleweed-choked fences in winter and carried tons of topsoil from cultivated farmland in summer.

On one such day when Bob was raking straw with the Percheron mares, the wind came up, the sky turned black and I ran out to the field to grab Dolly's halter to lead the horses to shelter. It was so dark with flying topsoil that Bob couldn't even find the gate!

## AN IDEAL CHILDHOOD

Bob and I really were "bush babies" as our mom called us, because we loved to wander out into the back-forty pasture. One time when we were quite young our mom handed us a small bowl and told us to go fill it with wild strawberries. We headed for the pasture, where we knew they grew best, and picked the bowl full. Then, being kids, we proceeded to build a house out of the young, three-foot-tall poplars that were in the field. We discovered that we just had to break them partway so they would bend toward each other to form a shelter.

We needed a thick roof, I decided, so we broke off some leafier poplars to lie across the top. We were so busy playing and building that we didn't think to look up at the sky.

We crawled inside our little house to eat our bowl of berries and we sat there, full and happy, as we watched a tiny green worm crawling among the leaves in our roof.

But suddenly, that prairie sky opened up. We could hear the rain pouring down, but we were sitting snug in our house, which wasn't leaking too badly, so we weren't concerned. Soon the cloudburst passed on and our mom came sloshing through the mud calling to us. She was so surprised and relieved to find us reasonably dry. She had brought coats, which we put on, and we followed her home for lunch.

She stopped worrying about us after that. She knew we would be okay outside on our own exploring, and there were no predatory animals in that area for her to be nervous about. From then on, our summers were spent having outdoor adventures.

As we grew, so did our talent for building shelters. When we were six and eight years old we built a teepee by cutting down twelve-foot poplars with my hatchet. We limbed them and stood them up like a teepee. It had too much daylight coming through, so I thought of a remedy: creeping cedar! It had lots of needles, and it "crept" along the ground like horizontal vines.

We found a patch and chopped off a pile of it, but it was too much to carry. We went looking for the mares, Queenie and Dolly. I led Queenie to our pile by tying a length of the creeping cedar around her neck. Bob held her while I piled the six-foot-long vines across her back. We interwove the vines through the poles of the teepee, closing most of the gaps up to about five feet high. It was a credible shelter. Now that we had laid claim to a piece of our jungle, we decided to trap ourselves an elephant!

We borrowed a spade from the garden, and worked very hard at digging our pit. When it was about three feet deep, we laid dry sticks across it and piled dry grass onto them. Our trap blended in with the pasture grass.

Weary but happy, we went home to lunch, satisfied we'd have an elephant on our return. However, the neighbour across the road had heard us working there, and he was waiting for us when we returned to check our elephant trap. He bawled us out, told us a horse could fall into our pit and made us fill it in while he stood there. We were resentful, naturally, as we hadn't caught our elephant yet ...

While our wild imaginations got us in trouble from time to time, our hearts were in the right place. Once, for our mom's birthday, my brother and I caught a jarful of fireflies at twilight, then crept into the house and threw them around the darkened room, yelling: "Happy birthday, Mom!"

## FIRST BUSINESS VENTURES

The Great Depression hit us prairie people when I was seven. While we were doing fine on the farm because of our big garden and our chickens and cows, I soon realized that if I wanted any money of my own, I'd have to make it myself.

That spring a government project was launched throughout the prairie schools to help farmers save thousands of bushels of wheat that were being "harvested"—and eaten—by gophers and crows. So Bob and I set to work drowning gophers for their tails and collecting crows' eggs and feet.

Our teacher tallied the points we had gained from our energetic hunts and they accumulated to being worth fifty cents. This would be our Christmas money, we decided, and we used it to buy Mom a pretty apron by mail order from the Eaton's fifteen-cent page. It arrived all in pieces that she sewed together by hand. There were ties around the waist, and a pocket too. We were pretty happy.

When I was ten, I made my own pocket money by snaring jackrabbits in winter. Their trails were everywhere in the snow, crossing the prairie and dodging under barbed-wire fences. The rabbits all used the same trails.

Bob and I made snares from the wire wrapping on old corn brooms, as it was light, malleable and strong. We learned to hang our wire loops at the right height to catch the rabbit around his neck.

Every day after school, we checked our trapline. When we had stockpiled a dozen or more rabbits, a kind farmer offered to take our rabbits—and me—by team and sleigh to the local fox farm. I remember him teasing me about his commission as we squeaked and jingled along the two miles over the sparkling landscape, standing in the open sleigh box. I sold our jackrabbits for fifteen cents apiece, which meant we were rich!

At that time my teacher at school was giving us art lessons using lots of colourful paint. My girlfriend and I had run out of paint, which we had to buy ourselves, and we needed new boxes of Reeves watercolours, but we didn't have any money. So I came up with a plan.

I knew the garage mechanics in town always needed rags to wipe their hands on while monkeywrenching. So I figured we should go get some and sell them to the mechanics. My friend and I went door to door making our pitch to the nice housewives, who shared their rag collections with us for free. The mechanics were astonished by our perspicacity, and they paid us fifty cents a bag. We cleared one dollar and fifty cents, and our paint boxes were seventy-five cents apiece.

My ventures didn't always work out for the best—another money-maker I discovered, by asking a farmer, was collecting ripe clover seed by hand. I stripped the seed from the stalks into quart jars at fifteen cents a quart. But because I didn't own any gloves, my fingers soon became raw to the point of bleeding. I gave up this scheme and went home to doctor my hands. Mom had to rub

Vaseline into them and wrap them in dishtowels.

When summer offered the opportunity, I often went berry picking. Saskatoon berries were plentiful where we lived. One day when I was about fourteen, I had filled a galvanized milking pail and was trudging home the two miles when a sudden thunderstorm roared in. I was nowhere near shelter and was exposed out on the bald prairie. The only protection was a cutbank at the roadside. I rolled under the sod overhang to escape the marble-sized hailstones crashing and bouncing all around me.

I was safe under there but my berries weren't so lucky, as there was no room for the bucket in my little shelter. When the storm moved on, with lightning flashes and muttering thunder, I crawled out to inspect my berries. Sure enough, they were just a bucket of mush.

I went out again the next day to pick a patch the storm had missed. I sold the fat, washed berries to a hotel restaurant, telling them they could use them for pies, at fifteen cents a quart. I used the berry money to buy a pair of Cuban-heeled black dress shoes, which were all the rage then at school.

My high school class. I am on the bottom left.

In high school my friends called me "Frisky" because I was so athletic. By then, after all the years at the farm, I could ride horseback like the wind and I played sports too, especially softball. I was captain of the girls' team and was sent to a city sports day to represent my school. I won a few ribbons that day. The older kids would put on Saturday night dances at our school and we would hold polka competitions. I loved to dance and my partner and I always won out over everyone else.

I was an avid reader, and my favourite book was *The Swiss Family Robinson*. I imagined living the adventures described in that book, but tailored mine to fit my life on the Alberta prairie. When I learned about other places in Canada that didn't have these big windstorms or hailstorms, I was fascinated. I read about huge grasslands where ranchers raised cattle, where coniferous timber grew and provided shelter and logs for building cabins. Where mountain ranges stood ten thousand feet tall against blue sky, patched with snowbanks that lasted all summer, and herds of deer or moose roamed. And all of this was right next door in British Columbia.

My daydreams created a lifestyle I was determined to experience for myself—someday.

## VENTURING INTO THE WORLD

When I was sixteen, my mom bought me a lovely filly—a sorrel, of Kentucky Whip breeding—and I trained her for a year before looking for a cowboying job for us. The job I found was just perfect. A neighbouring rancher had a pasturing-by-day herd that had a penchant for pushing down the barbed-wire fence protecting a lush, green oat crop. My job—and my new horse Tucky's—was to herd them away from that fence.

I'd pack a lunch, and when the cowherd was under control, Tucky and I dined: her on grass and me on sandwiches. The pasture was treeless, so when Tucky rested, one hind leg akimbo, I lay on the ground in her shadow.

We spent July and August at this job. I made a total of forty dollars and decided I was now ready to go out into the world to seek my place in the Great Scheme of Things. I had worked hard at school and had done well. I decided to head west to Vancouver and made plans with my big sister, Mabel.

The night I was planning to catch the train and meet up in Edmonton with Mabel, who was twenty-two by then, there was a town dance. The train wouldn't leave until after midnight, so I told Mom I'd go to the dance to say goodbye to my school friends before the train left.

"Don't carry your money in your pocket," Mom advised me. "Put it into your stocking!" So I put twenty dollars under each foot, encased by my silk stockings, and danced on it for three hours. I realized later that probably wasn't what she meant ...

My gang of friends all came to the station to see me off. Some of them thought I was crazy, and some were intrigued by my courage. I said my goodbyes and got on the train, ready for my big adventure.

My friend Elsa and me in Vancouver. Elsa and I decided to change our names as a joke. Elsa became Jacquie and I changed my name from Ethel to Gerry. I preferred Gerry, so I kept it.

I met Mabel in Edmonton and we continued on to Vancouver. The train ride was exciting, and by daylight we were on the coast. Coming from the prairies, I had developed a passion for mountains, even though I had never seen any. I was thrilled to finally see them in person.

Mabel and I both got household jobs in Vancouver. Mine was as a governess to an adorable eighteen-month-old baby girl named Marianne. Her parents both worked, so I became her full-time custodian as well as helping out with the housework when possible. Two days into the job, the distraught mother received word that her mother in Toronto was to have her leg amputated due to cancer. Extremely upset, she asked me if I could run the household for a month, as her mother needed her immediately.

Without hesitation, I said, "Sure!"

Suddenly the job had expanded to include preparing meals along with everything else, so I was extremely busy. There were hosted dinners at which I served the courses while wearing a maid's uniform.

I had been cooking since I was twelve, so I knew how to manage things and was able to fit it all into a schedule that still left time for Marianne's hour-long buggy rides. Weeks passed, and the mother returned.

By then I longed for a return to farm life. Luckily, my brother Bob found me a summer job cooking on a ranch in the Chilcotin. I gave notice to my employers, telling them I would be back in the fall, and when it was time to go I hopped onto a boat to Squamish, where it connected with the Pacific Great Eastern (PGE) railway that served the BC Interior at Williams Lake.

I luxuriated in the ambiance of train travel. With my Brownie Hawkeye camera I snapped photos of the train going around bends and curves and took pictures of a roaring glacier-fed creek battling boulders and cascading right below my window. The wheels kept up a singsong, and to me it sounded like "You're heading to the mountains ..."

When I arrived in Williams Lake, I took a room at the Lakeview Hotel on Railway Avenue. The next morning, before leaving for the Chilcotin on the "Hodgson's Stage" (a two-ton truck driven by a man called Tommy Hodgson), I took a walk around the village. I saw Mackenzie's Store and the telegraph office, the Log Cabin Hotel, Moore's Store and a shoe-repair store. Fortified by a good breakfast at the Lakeview Café, I climbed into the cab of Tommy Hodgson's truck and headed west.

Fourteen miles along a dirt gravel road the truck came to the Fraser River—a mighty body of snowmelt water originating somewhere north and clearing the province of British Colombia in its head-on rush to the Pacific Ocean near Vancouver.

Spanning this huge, turbulent river was a strange-looking bridge. It had a hump in the middle with cables leading to both banks. Tommy geared down to make the curve onto the bridge's level, solid approach, but when the truck began going uphill my frantic heart was pounding in my ears.

Tommy kept up a stream of Irish banter as the centre span began to creak and sway, the narrow side railings doing little to hide the whitecapped, churning waters rushing beneath. Even though the truck was creeping carefully, the creaking and groaning of that cable-hung bridge increased loudly along with the swaying.

Jovial Tommy chuckled as he entertained me with some history of the area and his pre-bridge crossings of this Fraser River. He said that they used to cross upstream where the water was quieter, and travellers to the west side, or the Chilcotin side, had fought to cross when it wasn't at full flood. I was white-knuckled by now. I heaved a pent-up sigh of relief as the truck rolled down off the level span that connected safely to the west bank.

Then we began the two-mile-long climb uphill out of the canyon up a series of switchbacks with very tight corners—too tight to negotiate in on slow advance. Tommy had to stop, change gears and back up to re-align the front wheels with the road.

Coming from flat prairie country, this was a hair-raising experience for me. But we made it without misadventure and soon the country flattened out while the faithful truck growled along. Tommy grinned at me and hollered, "Welcome to the Chilcotin!"

I had never seen wide-open, unfenced grasslands like the

ones I saw then. There was a stretch that Tommy called Beecher's Prairie, and then another he called Hance's Timber, because he said Mr. Tom Hance had cut a road through it by hand with his axe.

We started down a narrow, twisting, steep sidehill track overlooking a deep canyon that ended up at Hanceville, a guest ranch owned by the three Hance brothers, who also ran the post office, which put Hanceville on the map. We stopped there for the night and the Hance brothers were very cordial. They fed us and then showed us to our rooms.

The next day I arrived at the Dick Church Ranch at Big Creek, where I would be working for the summer. My job would be to help Mrs. Church with the housework, as well as feed a crew of ranch labourers and look after the children, who were six and four.

I really enjoyed the job and liked looking after the two little ones. On Sundays I could ride one of their horses, and even cowboy a little.

Little did I know that my life was about to take its own direction.

The Churches' nineteen-year-old niece, Isobel Moore, stopped in overnight when she was trailing the horse herd belonging to her mother, Dolly Moore, to Minto City, a gold-mining town where Dolly had a horse-packing contract with Minto Mines.

Isobel (or Issy, as she liked to be called) and I got along famously right away, and we had a lot to talk about—she was living the very lifestyle that I longed for and had come to BC to find: living in the mountains and working with horses.

When Issy got back from her trip she went home to the Circle X Ranch in Tatlayoko and told her father, the owner of the ranch, about the girl she had just met who loved horses as much as she did. At his daughter's urging, Mr. Moore wrote me a letter offering a full-time one-year ranch job as companion to his exuberant daughter starting in the following May of 1940.

I was so excited. The seeds of my dream had been sown, and I had the promise of a job on a ranch in the mountains to look forward to the next spring. After the cattle shipping and haying was over at the Church Ranch, I returned to my other job in Vancouver to look after Marianne and her family until my new life started.

## BACK TO THE CHILCOTIN

In early May I left Vancouver for Tatlayoko and arrived safely, courtesy of Tommy Hodgson and his two-ton truck once again. When I first saw those nine-thousand-foot glacier-topped mountains bordering turquoise-blue Tatlayoko Lake, all I could say was, "Oh my gosh!" I was in heaven.

Mr. Moore was there to greet me with his tractor and trailer to take me to the Circle X Ranch. I thanked Tommy Hodgson, said goodbye and climbed into the trailer, and we were off. It was only about three miles south, which made that mountain range grow even higher as we approached. Everything was greening up and spring was very evident here, but the mountain peaks were still snow-covered.

We pulled up beside a rambling, one-storey log house. I was happy to see Issy again, and she showed me to my room. She showed me where to wash up as well—it was a pantry with shelves holding jars of preserves on one short wall and a washbasin, soap and towel on a bench along the opposite wall under a window. She carried the basin toward the kitchen area. At the back of the kitchen range was a large metal forty-five-gallon barrel on a bench with a tap. There was a pipe that ran into the stove and back out so they could use the hot water.

Issy explained that the ranch house had no running water, but they did have what they called "walking water" that was carried in from the well. The wastewater was carried out back to a pit. One of the important daily chores, I would learn, was to fill that forty-five-gallon barrel's open top every day, usually in the morning, so there was water. Issy ran some into the basin so I could freshen up from my travels.

Over lunch I got to know Mr. Moore, and I asked him about the interesting T-shape of the log house.

"Well, I built this first part for myself," he told me. "It's about twenty-six feet by thirty-five feet, big enough for a kitchen, living room and my office/bedroom walled off in the far end corner. Then a young couple came along, new to the country, and they wanted to ranch but needed someone to teach them. They offered to work for room and board if I would 'show them the ropes,' as a cowboy says.

"So I put them up in a Pioneer tent and we got busy building a cabin for them. They didn't look like rancher folks, but you never know. We laid the new log cabin out at right angles to mine, with an eight-foot gap between the two.

"Theirs was the same size and style as my own. We felled trees, cut them into logs and skidded them in with my work team. They peeled them, and we dried the logs out for ten days and then started building. We had the cabin up and roofed in ten days. They moved in and felt pretty proud, too."

I was entranced. "So how long did they stay?" I asked.

"The young feller tried hard, and he was willing as could be, but the long, cold winter discouraged him. They left in the spring to go south to pick fruit. Strawberries, I think. When they left I just closed up the gap between the two cabins to make a pantry and washroom, cut a door into the new cabin and I had me a 'hotel' for my friends to overnight in when the mail came twice a month." He explained that the small room became the first post office for Tatlayoko pre-1940 when he lobbied the federal government for one.

Mr. Moore had done many amazing things for the town, I learned that night. He told me that when there were finally enough children to start a school, he let the teacher and kids use his cabin while the six local fathers built Tatlayoko's first school, an all-log building that served at least three generations of kids from grade one to grade eight.

I was excited to be there and to learn how to ranch from someone so resourceful, who obviously always thought ahead to the future generations.

Isobel Moore and I became fast friends. She was a cowgirl, living the life I dreamed of. I didn't hesitate when she invited me to come visit her at the Circle X Ranch in the Chilcotin.

# LIFE ON THE
# CIRCLE X RANCH

Issy showed me the ropes, and I soon got to know the lay of the land. The range started right outside the gate, so Issy and I could saddle our horses and ride up the sidehills to check the cattle in an hour. With more time, and a pocket lunch, we would ride further south to check the whole herd. We transported block salt, which weighed fifty pounds each, by pack horse, and took them two at a time out where there was abundant grazing. This helped to keep the cattle together, because they would stay close so they could lick the salt. When the two blocks were licked away we would put another two blocks out about four miles further south. The cattle loved their salt with all that new spring grass, so they were easy to locate on the fir-timbered range.

The Homathko River water was channelled into ditches, which led out across the hayfields, so it was our job to help with the irrigating too. I enjoyed the shovel work that kept the flow going, as well as damming to create flood-irrigating, or clearing the ditch to move the water along.

It was beautiful there. By June the wild strawberries were ripening, the birds were singing and a soft, sweet breeze was blowing across the hayfields.

I took to ranch life immediatley. Isobel (Issy) and I spent hours riding the range.

Mr. Moore seemed happy with his girl crew of two, and Issy and I got along like sisters. Neither of us was afraid of a hard day's work. I was already a pretty fair cook, as well, and I really enjoyed making homemade bread, doughnuts, cookies, roasts and stews for the family.

## LEISURE TIME AT THE BUTLER DANCE

By the time the annual spring dance was announced, we had the cattle salted, the calves branded and out on the range and the irrigating well in hand, and we were ready to relax and enjoy ourselves.

Issy explained that every spring the Butler family, who lived west of us in a parallel valley, opened their ranch house for a dance after their own cattle were branded, salted and out on the range.

When I arrived in Tatlayoko, the community only consisted of about a half-dozen families, all of them raising cattle and trapping during the winter. There wasn't much to do for entertainment when the work was done, except the radio, when we had time to listen to it. That's why the Butlers' spring dance, held at their ranch over in a valley on Mosely Creek, was such an anticipated event.

The day of the dance, Issy and I left home right after the chores were done. We rode on a wagon pulled by Mr. Moore's tractor (I now called him KB), picking up neighbours along the way. The only other transportation was by saddle horse, which was a tiring full day's ride. All us women brought our dancing dresses and shoes along but wore jeans for the rough and dusty trip.

The Niut mountain range rose over nine thousand feet between our two valleys, so it took a while to get to the Butlers' ranch. First we had to go north to get out of our valley and around the end of that range, then south into their narrower valley, then along another long stretch of dusty road. It was okay, though, because the scenery was grand.

Music for the dance was provided by local men from each valley, and our local musician rancher, Joe Schuk, rode with us in KB's wagon that year too. Those who rode in on horseback unsaddled when they got to the ranch and turned their horses in to a pasture with a good crop of spring grass especially reserved for them. The Butlers had a big log house with a large living room. There was no shortage of food and homemade beet or dandelion wine.

The musicians tuned up their guitars, banjos, violins and accordions and the dance began!

All the women wore dresses so it was a riotous, colourful affair. The dances were varied, too: there were polkas, two-steps, a French minuet, square dances and waltzes when we needed to cool off.

Isobel and me (I am on th right).

We took time off for midnight supper and visiting, and then we went at it again. The children all came as well, as nobody wanted to babysit and miss the dance. When the kids got tired they were put to bed in a quieter end of the house.

Fifty percent of the men were bachelors, so the few unmarried young women (including Issy and me) were much in demand. Neither Issy nor I were smokers or drinkers, but we sure loved to dance, and we could do every dance they called for.

At daylight, those who lived furthest away said goodbye, while the rest had coffee and breakfast and kept on dancing until it was finally time to go in the afternoon.

It was great fun, and the perfect initiation to the ways of the West.

## PLANS FOR IMPROVEMENT

KB's cattle range extended south between Tatlayoko Lake and the Potato Mountain cliffs for about eighteen miles and was about two or two and a half miles wide. We decided that Issy and I needed a cabin on the south end to provide shelter for the unavoidable overnighting when we were doing our range riding as the cattle drifted south and it became too far to ride back to the ranch. A cabin would keep us warm and safe from bears, wolves and cougars, and KB heartily approved of the idea.

He suggested that we girls had enough time to build the cabin right after the Butlers' dance, so we began collecting tools and making a list of what groceries we would need for ten days. But this plan didn't turn out quite like we thought it would ...

Very soon after arriving at the Circle X Ranch I had bought myself a horse, a four-year-old gelding that I named Gypsy. He was supposed to be broke, or "partly broke," to ride. One day I had saddled him up to go riding with Issy along the beach of Tatlayoko Lake.

He began bucking and running up and down on the sand dunes and the beach, with me holding on. I finally got him stopped without getting bucked off, which made him a little better behaved.

But just after the dance at the Butlers', some friends of Issy's drove into the ranch yard when we were home. Issy walked over to talk, then called to me, saying, "Hey Gerry! We can go for a car ride to Tatla Lake. We just have to milk the cows first."

A ride in a car? Wowee!

"I'll go get the cows right now," I said.

Gypsy was in the barnyard, so I bridled him—no time to saddle, as we were only going up into the nearby pasture. I led him into the pasture and jumped on bareback. "Come on, Gypsy, let's go get the cows," I said, and slapped him on the shoulder.

But right away, Gypsy lit into bucking, taking me by surprise. His hind feet kicked up high while he bogged his head, and as his head came up for the next lunge, his neck and my head collided with a shocking impact. I fell off, stunned. I just lay there seeing stars and trying to breathe.

When I recovered from the surprise and the dizziness I got unsteadily to my feet. Leading Gypsy, I herded the cows home into the corral, turned Gypsy loose and ran for the house.

As I ran past KB, he said, "Oh my gosh! Look at Gerry!"

I went to a mirror to see what he meant. My whole face had felt numb, and my shirtfront was blood-spattered. When I saw why, it was no wonder. My front teeth were smashed out. Well, all except one that was only half out.

I went to Tatla Lake all right … but it wasn't for a nice drive with Issy and her friends. It was to go to Williams Lake to find a dentist. After washing and changing my clothes, I was driven to Tatla Lake to catch the Hodgson truck returning to Williams Lake the next day.

I stayed at the Grahams' place in Tatla Lake, where I could only sip some warm soup for supper. Next morning when Tommy Hodgson came back from Anahim Lake, I got into the cab with him to go to Williams Lake. Tommy had so many stops to make picking up orders for the next week's delivery that we stopped for the night at Hanceville.

Again I had only a cup of soup, as I couldn't chew anything with that one half-out tooth. Next morning I heard that Grover Hance and his wife, Francie, were going into Williams Lake. Thinking they would get there sooner than Tommy, I asked if I could go with them, and they said, "Sure." I got into the back seat along with a young soldier who was returning from his furlough.

As Grover drove the dirt Chilcotin road, I noticed that he crowded the right side. I knew he had only one eye, so that explained it, but I began to worry about Sheep Creek Hill—that narrow, steep, long, twisty track down the side of the Fraser River Canyon. The corners on the switchbacks were so tight that truckers had to back up to get around them.

I devised a plan for survival. If I threw my arms out to brace myself on the floor I would be like a gyro-top: the outside would spin while the centre, which was me, stayed steady.

We started down the hill and approached a left-turning corner. Sure enough, Grover was hugging the extreme right edge of the gravel road. He got onto loose gravel, it carried him to the edge of the hill and over we went!

I automatically threw my hands wide on the ceiling, and my feet wide on the floor. My whole body was rigid. We went over onto our right side, fortunately, and not nose-first. We flipped three times and then crashed, coming to a stop lying on our right side.

The sudden stop jarred me loose, and I fell with my knees breaking the back-seat window.

Grover climbed up out of the driver's side door, which was now above him. Francie was lying in a heap on her side. He said, "Hang on, Francie! I'll cut the roof open and get you out!" It was a fabric roof, so it was a good plan.

But Francie didn't agree, even under the circumstances. "No #$^% way!" she said. "You are not wrecking our car." She crawled out the top door, tough lady that she was.

The soldier and I climbed out the back left door. We had come to a stop on a treeless, grassy level spot. Luckily we were both unhurt. My half-out tooth wasn't even knocked out.

All four of us were standing there when a two-ton truck geared and braked to a stop up above us on the road.

"Want a ride?" Tommy Hodgson called down with a grin.

We helped the injured Francie up the steep bank and into the back of the truck. I was sure my face was red from embarrassment after choosing to ride with Grover instead of Tommy. There were a few flat mailbags on the floor of the truck, and Grover stacked them for Francie to sit on.

Fourteen miles after crossing the suspension bridge, Tommy pulled up at the hospital in Williams Lake. He asked for a wheelchair for Francie, but she refused it and walked in. We heard later that she was badly busted up on her right side. Every roll threw her against the door, and her right ribs and arm were broken as well as her shoulder and collarbone. She didn't cry or complain at all. I surely admired how stoic she was.

Tommy told me where to go to get my last tooth pulled. A Dr. Mackenzie had rented rooms upstairs in the Log Cabin Hotel, and he pulled teeth and castrated dogs and cats, as a sort of town veterinarian. After he pulled it, I finally ate a chewable meal.

The Hodgson family invited me to stay with them so I could go back out west with Tommy, as his next run was into Tatlayoko. After my mouth was healed, I got an appointment with a dentist who made bridgework to replace my missing teeth.

## THE RANGE RIDERS BUILD A LOG CABIN

I finally made it back to the Circle X after my big adventure. KB and Issy were glad I had returned but were pretty shocked to hear about me rolling off of Sheep Creek Hill with Grover Hance.

They had been busy putting together all the equipment and food Issy and I would need during the week or so it would take to build the range cabin, which we decided should be about twelve miles down range. We left on horseback the next day, leading gentle Monty, the stallion. He was wearing his work harness and two pack boxes full of tools and vegetables, while his companion, a trusted pack mare, carried the bread, eggs and other food as well as some pots, sleeping bags and a tent.

We rode the twelve miles to where the cattle had drifted. There was a mixture of timber there, including maple, fir and some lodgepole pine (log-cabin-building size), as well as a nice cold spring surrounded by willows. We unpacked, staked and hobbled the horses, built a cooking fire, set up our tent and rolled out our bedding, and we were "home."

This was all new and delightful to me: the big, beautiful trees, the smell of the campfire smoke, horses chomping on the grass. There were even a few curious Circle X cows that came to visit.

After a quick supper, we found a site for our cabin close to a stand of trees that were the right size for our project. Issy, myself and the collie dog, Ring (named for the white fur collar he wore), slept peacefully with an overnight log on the fire and Issy's 30-30 rifle close at hand to protect us.

We were up with the birds. We restaked the horses, made bacon and eggs and coffee and enjoyed our breakfast while Ring had his dog food and a meaty beef bone for dessert.

Issy undercut the trees with an axe, and then we both used a crosscut saw to fall them. We had five trees down, limbed and skidded to our cabin site by Monty when we stopped to make lunch and water the staked horses.

After lunch we peeled our logs with a drawknife, then found some flat rocks to set them on, and the first round of our little eight-by-ten-foot cabin was arranged! We left the new logs to dry in the sun, and Issy suggested we put up a high horizontal pole near camp.

"What's that for?" I asked.

"It's a strong pole high up off the ground resting on tree branches," Issy said. "It's to hang our food from whenever we leave camp so bears and coyotes and other animals can't get at it."

That made sense to me, so we found a dry, light, dead pine, cut it down, limbed it, roped one end and hauled it up over a limb with Monty's help. Issy climbed the fir tree to guide the pole to rest on a low limb. Then she wired it there, removed our rope, came down and snared the other end. She climbed a tree about ten feet from the first, looped the rope around it above a strong limb and told me to "haul 'er up," which meant, "Hook Monty to the rope end." He didn't mind at all.

In ten minutes the pole hung horizontally, and Issy guided its end over the limb. She anchored it there, also with a length of haywire, as she had done with the first end.

"Now," she said, recoiling her lariat rope, "we can safely ride off to check on our cattle without worrying about our food."

We tossed a rope over the pole and hauled up a food box, and then we celebrated with coffee and home-cooked doughnuts. I sure was enjoying this bush living.

By the third day we had enough logs hauled in and peeled to make the walls. We left them decked to dry in the sun. While Issy watered and restaked Monty and the mare, I saddled our two mounts. We needed to ride south about ten miles to check the range cows.

This hillside overlooked Tatlayoko Lake, which was turquoise blue with small whitecaps, signifying south winds. As it was early June, the grass was lush and the flowers were blooming, including the bright balsamroot, which were big, wild sunflowers. All the cattle were asleep and content, their fast-growing calves frolicking among them.

There was no grizzly sign—they would be following the snowmelt up the mountain slopes to feast on wild potatoes and hoary marmots. We sat our horses in the warm June sun, listening in the silence for the cries of crows, whose raucous cawing almost always signifies the location of a dead animal. But all was still.

After a while we turned our horses toward camp, happy to have had a day of rest while still doing our job and checking on the cattle.

The next day we rode the hillsides nearby to search for loners and stragglers, which were stray cattle, so we could start them south to join the main herd, where the bulls and the salt were.

By now our cabin logs had dried enough to continue building the walls. We notched each corner to hold the next log securely as we built the walls steadily higher up to seven and a half feet in case we would need a floor later. Then we needed a ridgepole to support the smaller logs for roofing, and we were finished.

That evening we carried our bedding into our new range cabin. We folded our tent to pack out in the morning and built a small fire inside the cabin ringed around with stones. The smoke went up and out of the gap we left in the roof for that purpose, aided by the cold air coming in under the bottom logs. We hung a tarp over the open doorway. Our mattresses of fir branches thick with needles smelled great.

It wasn't fancy, but the cabin was protection from animals and the elements. Later we would bring some boards, nails and hinges on Monty and build a door. It was a summertime cabin, so it didn't require chinking.

The next morning we packed up our camp and rode our saddle horses toward home, leading Monty and the mare. We had accomplished what we set out to do, and all within the allotted week. KB was glad to see us, and he hadn't started worrying yet. He enjoyed hearing all about our cabin building, and he complimented us for the job we had done.

## TRAILING DOLLY'S HORSES TO MINTO

Soon KB reminded Issy to start getting ready because it was almost time for trailing the big horse herd through the South Chilcotin mountains to Issy's mother, Dolly, which was what Issy had been doing when I met her the summer before.

Isobel had a way with animals. She was a great cow boss and a good teacher.

But first Issy, being a responsible "cow boss," decided to pack a good supply of salt down range because we would be gone a week and without salt the cattle would scatter.

So we loaded three horses with two blocks apiece and rode as far as our range cabin. Early the next morning we packed one horse with two blocks to go further down range to the cattle, leaving the other two horses staked and the four spare blocks stored in the cabin covered with a tarp. We barricaded the door so nothing could get in and we set off, eating the beef sandwiches I had brought from home as we rode.

Everything was okay with the cattle except that they were out of salt, so they were sure glad to see us. We made it home that evening to a hot meal and soft beds. The next morning I mixed up and baked a big batch of bread, some for KB, and some for us to take with us on our trip to Minto. I also brought homemade butter and canned fruit, rolled oats and bacon.

We left the ranch trailing our herd of two dozen horses. Issy took the lead, as she knew the route. She led the two horses that were packing camping gear, and I hazed the remaining twenty head along.

We camped most nights on the way down, except for one or two when we stayed with friends. We went by way of Big Creek, through Graveyard Valley, and the snow-choked pass out of Graveyard was difficult. We got off to lead our saddle horses, but they were lunging and plunging in the big snowdrift, trying to climb onto us. The snow held me and Issy on foot, but not them. We ran fast out in front to avoid their feet while leading them, with the leaders breaking trail.

On the protected side of the ridge, a huge drift had been built over the winter by fierce winds hurling the snow from the bare south mountainside over the ridge. Eventually we broke over the ridge and saw bare ground and bright yellow sunflowers. The scenery was spectacular. We camped that night at Spruce Lake. Our campfire was cozy, and we kept it burning all night since we were in bear country.

When we got to Minto the next day, Dolly was happy to see her daughter and her beloved horses arrive, and I was introduced to Issy's brother Bev, who was eighteen.

After a couple of days of visiting, Issy and I needed to get home to check the range cows and start haying, so we caught the PGE train with our bridles and saddles all the way back to Williams Lake. From there we were lucky enough to catch Tommy Hodgson and get a ride to Tatlayoko.

Haying was a lot of fun, I discovered. I did all the cooking for the teamsters and the pitchfork crew. We used horses to cut the hay, rack it, haul the slip loads (a hayrack on skids) to the hay sheds and pull the cable that hauled the sling loads up to be dumped in the big shed with walls. After lunch I would hurry with the dishes so I could go out and pitch hay into the haycocks. It was clover and timothy hay, and the air smelled marvellous in our valley.

When the haying was finished, the crew all moved up to KB's thousand-acre Skinner Meadow to cut and stack the wild hay that was growing naturally. This was a different style of haying, since it was stacked out in the open by a professional who knew how to build a weatherproof stack. The hay must be tramped and packed in the middle, with all the sides smoothly sloping out and down to shed water. I learned the system from KB, and five years later I too could build a stack that didn't leak.

## My First Beef Drive

It was September now, and no sooner was haying over than it was time to gather in the cows to separate them for market. We divided them into the yearling steers, the culled yearling heifers, the old cows (ten to twelve years old) and the bulls we needed to replace. With only the one range, we needed new bulls every two years, and we often traded bulls with other ranchers. Our bulls went out to range with the cows in June, and the calves were born the following March. Issy and I were taking on the beef drive, and I just knew I was going to experience some high adventure! Whooee!

We checked the date of the sale in Williams Lake and allowed ourselves twenty days to get there. We would be walking our herd an average of ten miles a day. We took three pack horses to carry camp necessities, but we also packed our ball gowns, silk stockings and dancing shoes in pillowcases. The town would be putting on a dance and other activities for Klondike Night while we were there, to show appreciation for the ranching industry. It was sure to be a good time.

When we first started out we needed extra help to drive the herd the first two days, as the young stock would break away to run back home, but by the third day they trailed better. By the fifth day they were such a cohesive bunch that we could drive through a herd of strange cattle and come out on the other side with all of our animals drifting placidly in a perfect wedge shape, following their chosen leader, who was usually an old cow. Some ranchers

In the winter we had to supplement the calves' feed with grain.

take the leader back home to head up another drive, as they can be worth several cowboys.

The agricultural department of the government provided a few fenced pastures along the Chilcotin Road, which would be handy once we reached the road, but at first we were going across country, following parallel to the Chilko River. There was a wagon road that kept the herd within sight, but the rest was pine forest until we finally came out onto a grassy meadow that they could graze on.

On the fifth day we had been travelling since daylight, so we were happy for the break. We could now unpack and unsaddle to rest and graze the horses while we made breakfast. We knew the cows would graze for about an hour, and when they had filled all of their cud pockets they would lie around for another hour chewing their cuds before they got restless. We had plenty of time to enjoy a breakfast of sandwiches, but we couldn't make coffee because we were on a grassy meadow and couldn't build a fire.

On this drive there were two old corrals on the meadows known as Broken Sleigh and Rawhide. One had a slough with water for the cattle; the other had no water. We put the herd into the corrals at dusk, which gave us an undisturbed sleep. But because one group had to be watered, we had to let the thirsty animals out as soon as it was light enough to see them in the morning and herd them down that wagon trail.

They walked so fast that one of us had to ride point in the lead to slow them down! Once we reached a creek where the cattle and the horses could tank up, we were all happy again and we continued meandering along on our journey.

It was autumn and the poplars were golden and beautiful, but the wasps were armed and ready. They had built their hives in the rotten logs that lay on the trail, and whenever the cattle disturbed a nest they'd stop at the sound of the buzzing and then the ones that got stung would explode from the herd and they'd run in all directions. The rest would panic and run away too. We had to be watchful and get the jump on the cattle before they disappeared into the forest.

Six days later, when our trail finally came out to join the Chilcotin Road, which was still only a dirt road, we gave our herd a day's rest. The next day would be sixteen miles long, all the way to Bull Canyon.

The canyon got its name because it was an ideal pasture where the local ranchers could all keep their bulls. It was large and bordered by the Chilcotin River on one side and steep cliffs on the other. There was a bit of fence and a cattle guard with a gate at each end. The ranchers used it until turnout date, which was June 15, so they weren't using it now.

Issy and I put the herd in the cattle guard and then we allowed ourselves a much-needed break. We rode four miles to Alexis Creek to eat at a restaurant and go to a six o'clock movie, which was a big treat for us.

The theatre was a large meeting room over a store. It had a level floor and lots of chairs, which were mostly occupied by Native women and children dressed in bright cotton dresses and moccasins. Issy told me there was a reservation nearby.

The movie was a jerky black and white western. The young children were very loud and some of them were crying so loudly that we couldn't hear the dialogue, but no matter, we still had a wonderful time. We rode back to camp before dark so we would be ready to drive our herd through the village in the morning.

When we set out again the next day we were about halfway to Williams Lake and right on schedule. A lot of the road we were travelling was unfenced, open range with abundant grass, creeks and ponds. We made use of the government pastures, which were free to ranchers, when we could.

The treacherous suspension bridge over the Fraser River canyon would be our next difficult obstacle. The rule was to take only fifteen head across at a time to prevent putting strain on the bridge. We cut out fifteen head and drove them onto the suspended section, which was solidly attached to the cliff.

Another cattle drive had obviously gone through the day before, as there was a trail of cow manure down the centre of the bridge. We could see the movement of the river through the railing, and the roaring below unnerved the cattle. They reversed ends, and we had to yell and smack them with our lariats to turn them and move them forward. I went in the lead to give them something to follow, while Issy and her collie crowded them along to the section that curved upward. As soon as we moved onto it, the bridge began to shake, wriggle, squeak and bang. I forced my terrified horse to move along one step at a time.

The cattle now strung out single file, too scared to crowd the side rails where they could see the river rushing below. We reached the top of the curve and started down the slope, and by now my horse and line of cows were staggering like drunken sailors.

We were only too happy to step onto the solid platform on the other side. We put that bunch of cows into the corral and went back for another fifteen head. We had to do it three times, all the while convinced those cables would let go and dump us into the river!

Once we were safely across and our herd was united, the cattle strung out on the easy uphill grade paralleling the river. We only had fourteen miles to go before we got to town and the stockyards.

We camped that night at the McKays' Four-Mile Ranch. We were close then, and we rode horseback up to the town to rent a cabin at Mrs. Hendry's auto court for the week. There was plenty of grazing for tethered horses near the cabins.

The sale went on for two days. Our cattle were sorted into yearling steers, yearling heifers, cows and bulls, cut from our herd by the stockyard riders, weighed and released into the show ring where the auctioneer read off the pertinent info such as breed, sex, age, owner and brand. Then he launched into his fast singsong jargon interspersed with slowly increasing bids, new offers of so many cents per pound of bodyweight. His spotters were sharp-eyed stockmen, and they yelled out as buyers signalled their acceptance of the increased bid.

This went on as long as it took to sell approximately three thousand head of Chilcotin and Cariboo cattle being marketed at that October sale. We were excited to win the silver loving cup for the best group of ten Hereford yearling steers.

The sale was followed by a big dinner with guest speakers, followed by the whoop-de-do they called Klondike Night in appreciation of the local ranching industry, which had been the major industry in that region in the 1930s and '40s. Now Issy and I could shuck our jeans and cowboy boots and don our floor-length ball gowns and dancing shoes for the much-anticipated, and much-deserved, night on the town.

The band assembled and tuned up, the tables were removed and the dancing began. Booths along both walls offered games like darts, ring toss and roulette wheels. Everyone had to buy "Klondike money," which was the only acceptable legal tender that night.

Issy and I danced the night away and had a grand evening. We didn't drink, as I was always a teetotaller, so we were alert and ready next morning to bank the cattle cheques and pay our bills with Mrs. Hendry and Mackenzie's General Store. We ordered supplies of winter imperishables, like one-hundred-pound sacks of flour, sugar and rice, cases of dried prunes, apricots, peaches and apples, and cases of canned tomatoes to be hauled out to the ranch by Tommy Hodgson's freight truck.

Our dancing duds were rewrapped in the pillowcases and we got back into our denim jeans and cowboy boots and headed back west. It would take us six or seven days.

We had a lot to do, and October was fast disappearing. We had cattle to round up, a garden to dig up and store in the root cellar and a huge supply of wood to harvest before winter.

## GETTING READY FOR WINTER

Issy and I and our weary saddle horses were glad to return home when we finally arrived back at the Circle X on October 20.

After a day of resting up and exchanging the month's highlights with Issy's father, we got to work. First on the list was the garden. With three of us digging up the potatoes, turnips, carrots and beets, we had it all into the root cellar by the second day.

Next, us two cowgirls scoured the range for any cattle that had not drifted up to the Skinner Meadow, which was their winter

Kennon Beverly Moore (KB) served in WWI. He was my mentor and friend and eventually a grandfather to my children.

feeding grounds, six miles from the ranch. Once we got them rounded up and onto that big meadow, we could concentrate on getting the winter wood supply. Jack pine is limby, but lodgepole pine, so called because it grows tall and straight with few limbs on the trunk, was the preferred firewood. We felled them with axes or crosscut saws, and I dragged the dead ones home with Roanie and Blackoby, the ranch horses, or the tractor if possible. If there was a dead fir handy we felled it and cut it into blocks about fifteen inches long, then wrapped a logging chain around the block and sat on it while the team skidded it to the woodpile. These blocks split easily into firewood and burned hot for quick meals on the cookstove.

In the evenings, once the chores were all done and supper dishes washed up, I liked to involve KB in conversation about where he came from and how he ended up in the valley. He was happy to oblige, and Issy was always interested too. Issy and I were fascinated with the family history and the stories about how the ranch came to be. Issy didn't know it all, because she had only recently been reunited with her father after being raised away from Tatlayoko by Dolly.

So with the fire crackling, and the naphtha-gas lamp hissing, he told us stories about being born and raised in Boston, Massachusetts. His family had come from Britain originally and some of them had actually founded Boston. Indeed, one Paul Blackstone

Moore had donated some of his own land to become a common cow pasture for the community's milk cows about five generations ago, so cattle ran in the family. "Now it is a park, known as the Boston Commons," KB said.

Mr. Moore's father, Beverly Kennon Moore, had been a wealthy lawyer until the Wall Street Crash. When young Kennon Beverly (KB) reached the age of fourteen, he left home, rode the freight trains west to Oregon, crossed the border into BC and worked at any job he could find so he could keep moving north. At Williams Lake he heard about the Chilcotin and got a job with a rancher named Norman Lee in Lees Corner, BC.

He saved up enough to buy a horse and saddle, then rode to Chezacut (a place there called Ken Moore's Flats attests to his temporary stopping off). But one nice, balmy spring day he took a ride to see more country and found his way into Tatlayoko Lake Valley. It was April, and the new grass was four inches high. He liked what he saw, staked out some acreage and proceeded to build a log cabin.

KB was Tatlayoko's first settler. Two or three others had come seeking gold, or to trap fur-bearing animals, but they didn't stay. In those days Bella Coola was inhabited by a Norwegian community, and among them was a guide outfitter named Ralph Edwards who hunted big coastal grizzly bears for very wealthy clients. He hired KB as his assistant, and after five years as an apprentice, KB acquired his own guide outfitter's licence and guided clients in Tatlayoko Valley. Between guiding and trapping, he built up a grubstake to buy livestock, but by then the First World War broke out.

KB volunteered, even though he was an American and his country wasn't involved yet. But he had chosen to live in Canada, so he went to war for Canada. He was assigned to the Royal Canadian Engineers, who laid track to carry pushcarts loaded with ammunition to the soldiers in the front trenches. The dreaded mustard gas, which was later outlawed, felled a lot of those soldiers, and many died. KB was gassed as well, and then was sent to Scotland to recuperate. "I was billeted with a family that made good Scotch whisky, so I could drink a pint a day," he told us, laughing. He credited his recovery to the whisky.

Eventually he returned home, married his fiancée, Dolly, and continued with his chosen life's work of building a cattle ranch. They had two children: Isobel and Beverly, his son who now lived with Dolly.

He told us how when he had first started building his Circle X Ranch after the war, he needed horses. There were herds of wild horses running around on government land. They were available to anyone with a fast saddle horse and a rope. The government was considering a program that would rid the Crown land of wild horses. They had multiplied in numbers to where they were really damaging these famous grasslands. There would be a bounty on them—three dollars for a pair of mare's ears, and five dollars for a pair of stallion's ears, plus the scrotum to prove it was a stallion. Anyone who could ride and shoot could sign up for this program.

The horses were easiest to catch in the spring. One day KB rode out to see what he could find. He wanted to catch a yearling, as it would be young enough to train. He knew that soon the wild horses would be gone from this piece of rangeland because of the bounty hunting.

He closed in on a small band and then lassoed a colt as it trailed behind the band of feral horses on the Eagle Lake rangeland. He had what he came for: a yearling.

There he was, miles from home, with a mangy, tick-infested, small red roan colt choking at the end of his rope. Undaunted, KB dismounted, and as the colt fell he tied its feet together, then eased the rope on its neck. "There you are, little fellow. Catch your breath now. You and I have a long trail ahead of us."

He fashioned a war bridle of softer rope on the colt's head before releasing his feet, then remounted his horse to teach the colt to lead. After a few futile lunges for freedom, which came up short with the rope snubbed to the saddle horn, the colt began to realize that play was hopeless.

With KB talking to him all the while, pulling him this way and that to either side, within twenty minutes the youngster was responding, so now they could start for the home ranch.

"Whatever are you going to do with THAT?" Dolly asked him scornfully the next morning.

The colt was such a frightened, miserable-looking little creature, ewe-necked, runty, knobby-kneed and with a big head and feet, but KB had looked into his eyes and seen the makings of a fine, big part-Belgian draft horse, with a kind and gentle nature.

"I'm going to train him to help me build this ranch," he said. And train him he did. With good food and gentle treatment, Roanie grew to be a 1,200-pound, well-muscled, all-around ranch horse, who could be ridden, packed or worked in harness.

Together, Roanie and KB cleared land, dragging stumps and debris into piles to be burned, then harrowed the rich ground smooth to raise the first hay crop and a larger garden. Together they went hunting in the fall for meat for the winter, Roanie backpacking it in, while his boss man walked along in the lead. Together they travelled the twenty-three miles to Graham's Country Store, returning late at night with coffee, sugar and flour.

The ranch took shape slowly as Roanie skidded in logs to add on to the cabin, then for a barn, chicken house, corral and fencing.

But Roanie needed a partner. KB attended a little rodeo held at Stuie and a black horse came out of the bucking chute, but he didn't buck! KB bought him for thirty dollars and led him home. He put him into a double harness with Roanie, who was glad of the company, and taught Blackoby what to do. KB named him for his banker in Williams Lake, who he claimed was also "mean and unreasonable."

Roanie made the trek to the cattle drive every fall for quite a few years. Sometimes KB put both horses into harness to pull the wagon, so he could bring home a load of freight such as groceries and other necessities. When Issy and Beverly were very young, before they left the ranch with their mother when their parents broke up, they loved their hairy friend Roanie and rode double on him in the barnyard.

## LEARNING TO TRAP

All the small ranchers did some trapping to augment their income, and I was eager to learn too. Hunting predators like wolves and coyotes for their hides was profitable during the winter. Cougar hides were profitable too, since the big cats were a nuisance that killed every type of livestock they could get to.

KB had a trapline that started right across the Homathko River and ran the full length of the fifteen-mile-long Tatlayoko Lake on the west side. It also extended northeast ten miles to take in Skinner Meadow.

Because I had snared and sold jackrabbits as a child, I was very interested in this huge wilderness trapline. KB took me with him to learn how to set traps, build a cubby and camouflage a large trap. Before long I was running a section of the trapline to give him a break from it.

He also taught me to shoot, first with a .22-calibre rifle used for taking squirrels.

I would eventually graduate to a 30-30 rifle with open sights for bigger game. But that November 1940, I shot my first mule deer buck with one .22 long-rifle shell. He was standing in a thicket, looking at me while I searched my pockets amongst string, matches and bobby-pins for that one shell! The deer was only twenty-five feet away.

Squirrels could be difficult because they move a lot, and it took patience to make a clean headshot. You had to be careful: the skins, dried on wood stretchers, were worth twenty-five cents each if shot in the head, but shot through the body they were almost worthless.

I became very good with my little single-shot .22 and I could skin squirrels quickly while they were still warm while I looked for another.

The early winter passed quickly, and when we needed entertainment there were dances in the little log schoolhouse. We used a windup phonograph for the music. At Christmas we attended the school's special holiday concert as well.

KB didn't always join Issy and me at the dances and house parties;

he would relax at the ranch listening to the boxing matches on the radio and stoking the fire.

Before we could go out dancing or visiting, Issy and I always had to make sure the cattle were fed. We kept the calves of the previous spring and the bulls in their separate field pastures.

KB had the biggest job, which was feeding the main herd of cattle, who were six miles away on Skinner Meadow. He would stay out there for the week, but would always come back on weekends if the weather was good. On Fridays he would put out an extra feed of hay for the next day and ride his horse home for the weekend, going back again early on Sunday.

When he came back for the weekend Issy and I would have a special meal ready for him. We always had lots to tell him, and he had stories as well. Sometimes Issy and I would make ice cream with real cream in the hand-turning freezer and have a cake baked to go with it. We baked bread for ourselves and KB as well, and usually had a lard pail of stew for him to take with him when

An afternoon picnic with my good friends. L—R Jim Bonner, Vera Witte (Bonner), me and Hazel Witte (Henry-Litterick).

55

The Witte family saved all their old cars. Duane Witte and I show off the horse buggy on the right.

he returned to the meadow. He was a good cook, too, and was especially skilled with making cornbread and bannock.

Sometimes on nice days during the week, Issy and I would saddle up our horses and ride up the road to visit a neighbour or surprise her dad by showing up at the meadow with a batch of gingersnaps.

We were like one happy family. KB was so proud of his daughter, and he treated me very well too, which was so nice because I had lost my own father at such a young age. I was learning through this family how much a dad could contribute to the whole picture.

KB was a very social person, and he enjoyed having his neighbours drop by. He always loaned them anything they needed, if he had it. I would sometimes see huge rack-loads of his top-quality clover hay being hauled out of his gate with only a wave from the neighbour who was taking it, who would just shout, "Thanks, Ken! Till you are better paid." Which he never was.

The Native people liked KB very much too, and they would ride horseback twenty miles to visit him on mail days, which were twice a month. They would often stay for a day or two and share the news they had heard via the "moccasin telegraph."

## THE ARRIVAL OF BEVERLY MOORE

That January we had a surprise. During the week, while KB was out at Skinner Meadow with the cattle, his son, Beverly, showed up at the Circle X with the Hodgson mail truck.

Issy was happy to see her brother and we were excited to show KB his surprise when he got home on the weekend. Sure enough, he was very pleased and proud to have both of his offspring there under his own roof after so many years.

Issy and I figured that Bev, who was eighteen, must have missed his sister when he got news of all the fun we were having. We guessed that he probably felt left out and decided he would come up and check it out.

Bev intended to stay awhile and help out, and he got right in with the program, helping KB with the feeding of the cattle and extra horses at Skinner Meadow. At first they both came home on weekends together, but soon they took turns so someone was always with the cattle. It was nice for Issy and me to have help feeding the calves and bulls at home. Bev's willingness to pitch in was welcome, and we soon had the ranching chores well organized with all this extra help.

We didn't have any way to move the snow when it came, and sometimes we would get three feet overnight. When that happened we trampled out a big circle with our horses pulling the slip, and the cattle would follow and pack into a feeding area.

That winter, Issy, Bev and I had a wonderful time going by saddle horses or horse-drawn sleigh to house parties where we played games, shared news and had potluck dinners.

Sometimes on nice winter days we would clean off a patch of ice and have a hockey game with the neighbours, usually on the lagoon alongside Tatlayoko Lake, as the lake itself seldom froze. We could get chinooks in the middle of winter and then we could see the temperature change from −38°F to +60°F in five hours! Even if the lake did freeze over, it was never safe.

Spring came in with a warm wind licking up the snow and our spirits rose. It was time for the cows to come home from the big meadow, and they knew it. They were becoming restless, because they always calved at the home ranch where they could eat the clover hay.

There was still lots of snow at the meadow but the wild geese were honking and winging overhead in formation, the ducks were noisily congregating on ponds and the robins were gathering into groups to warble Old Man Winter into a timely grave.

With the brisk March air I could feel the throb and pulse of new ambitions being born, the growing excitement of working with the cattle, finishing that crucial section of fence that early snow had put a stop to. I realized how blessed we were in Canada to have these four distinct seasons. They may have controlled our lives, but they sure made life interesting.

Now that Bev was home, life was easier for KB. Bev was a tall young man at six foot two inches, and very strong. The two of them could work together to do things like repair the log fences once the wood had dried out from the snow.

It hadn't been easy for KB to operate the ranch alone all those years before Issy and I had come. In fact, he had been negotiating a deal with a landowner down in New Mexico to trade properties before Issy came back to help him. KB's brother, Paul, and his family lived down there and KB had not seen him or their sisters in forty years. He just never had enough time to get away from the ranch.

But then his daughter came home and now his son was here too. KB seemed to have a new lease on life. Despite his sixty years he seemed younger and more energetic than he had when I got there, and he put more energy into his work and making plans. Now that his kids were back, the future looked rosy.

## THE BIG ROAN COW

It was time for the main herd to come back to the ranch from Skinner Meadow to calve. The men were busy, so I volunteered to bring the cowherd home. It wasn't difficult; I rode my horse up to the meadow, opened the gate, scattered some hay along the trail and got behind them yelling, "Come on girls, let's go home!"

They went out for the hay and kept on going. They knew what to do. I made sure every cow went out of the gate before I closed it and followed behind. It was a joyful experience to see that herd of about two hundred good-looking Herefords with their red bodies, white faces and tail switches marching down that high road that was still covered in snow. The Coast Range was on the horizon, sparkling in the sunshine.

When they reached the valley road there was no stopping them, as they knew the good clover hay awaited them. That is, all but one big, red roan cow. She lay down and refused to get up, as she was heavy with calf. We were within a half mile of the ranch, and I left her to follow along once she had rested up a bit. I went on to push the stragglers along the road toward home.

KB was at the ranch yard to count the cattle on their way to the south fields where that sweet hay awaited them. He looked very pleased to watch the fruits of his labours striding by. But I was worried about the roan cow. As boss cowboy, I explained the situation to KB, who agreed that she needed to be brought home. He harnessed his trusted team, Roanie and Blackoby, and hitched them to the stoneboat, and KB, Bev and I rode up the road to fetch the cow.

There she was, still sitting comfortably on the road, head up, watching us arrive. Her look clearly said, "What took you so long?" We pulled up alongside her and wrestled her onto the stoneboat. KB drove, while Bev and I walked. She was a big cow, over one thousand pounds with the calf she was carrying, so the horses had a load to pull. She sat with her knees tucked in, looking very regal.

They brought her right into the hayshed that was attached to the barn and skidded her off onto a bed of hay. After putting the team and stoneboat away, we brought her a couple of buckets of water. She drank them down and continued eating hay. We left her to rest, sure that she would get up on her own.

But the next morning she was still lying down, waiting for breakfast. The men rigged a sling and pulley from the overhead beams to get her standing. That helped her get up, but her heart wasn't in it, and as soon as they took off the sling, she dropped in a heap. We straightened her out and left her sitting and chewing her cud.

The men were grumbling. "Might as well shoot her and get it over with now. She's only going to die anyway," they said.

"Oh no," I said. "Please don't. You can see she's heavy with calf. Just give her a day or two. She'll have her calf and then she'll stand."

So they packed her water twice a day, turned her from side to side, fed her choice hay and grumbled all the while. To get them on my good side I fed the men nice meals, surprised them with cakes and cookies and told them things like, "We'll see her licking her calf in the morning." Issy was off on a holiday, so she wasn't there to back me up.

But after six days of "choring after that cow," their minds were made up. They were going to shoot her in the morning.

"Oh no, don't shoot her!" I blurted out. "She's going to have twins!" I wasn't sure, but I felt I needed to substantiate my convictions. And the truth was, she was still eating and drinking and she was clear-eyed and heads-up when I paid her a visit every day. "Where there's life, there's hope," I argued. I didn't want to give up on that cow.

On the second day of her new reprieve, Bev carried water to the cow and there was a big, wobbly roan bull calf in excellent shape staggering around the shed. The mother was still down, so we dropped the calf beside her, put a teat in his mouth and massaged his throat so he would drink. He caught on right away and proceeded to suck and swallow the colostrum, that thick milk so necessary to just-born calves.

KB had come to see the miracle, and he left again to do chores. The cow was labouring a bit, and Bev and I expected it was to expel the afterbirth, but then a red tail appeared. Bev reached in and got a grip on both flanks, and the cow—with Bev's help—birthed a little, red, white-faced heifer!

I literally jumped up and down, saying, "I told you she was expecting twins! Didn't I? Didn't I!?"

We dragged the heifer calf around to the mother cow's head so she could lick it off, and I ran to tell KB.

My status as a caring stockwoman gained a few points that day.

Soon after, the cow got up and nursed both her calves. We kept her in that shed for a week to give her and her calves time to become stronger before putting them in with the other new mothers and calves. She went out in the spring range with the rest and brought both of her calves home with her that fall.

## SPRING CALVES AND AN APRIL SURPRISE

When the calves started to be born, we took turns checking the cowherd hourly in their big field. There were a few trees for shelter but the fields were baring off, so the cows usually went off by themselves to calve. We rode horses to cover more of the field.

Once we found a cow partly lying on her calf, but we saved the baby. Another cow dropped her calf in a hole full of water. I spotted the cow standing off by herself while the rest were eating their hay for breakfast. I had the old truck that day so I drove over to have a look and saw a little white face barely out of the water. I yanked him out of there, dragged him along the grass on both of his sides to dry him and create some warmth from friction, then loaded him into the cab and drove home fast. I put him into the bathtub and ran warm water over him while rubbing him by hand. The water became chilled right away. I let it drain out while the warm water flowed onto the calf.

It must have taken a half hour before the calf warmed up. After I dried him with towels and wrapped him in a blanket, I laid him beside the heater to keep warm. When he revived enough to walk around in the living room I took him back to his mother to nurse so he could get the colostrum he needed to avoid pneumonia. I surely was glad that I had driven the truck to check the cattle! The ranch's income depended on our calf crop in the spring.

Ben Wilson was a true cowboy. Issy and Ben fell in love and they became a great ranching team.

The routine of spreading feed on the field every day and checking the calf crop went on at every cattle ranch until the range had greened up. Our range licence for turnout was the middle of May. We put the two-year-old heifers on a nearby area of our range, and the older cows further down range since they were experienced and required less checking.

Young calves are such a delight to watch; within a short time after being born, they are up on wobbly legs, nuzzling their mother for her warm, rich milk. Within an hour or two they are butting heads with other calves, or springing into action to run in circles around their mothers, bucking and kicking at a tuft of hay or up-turned sod.

March was turning out to be a nice month, warm breezes, mild nights and no more snow. We couldn't believe our good fortune.

But on April 3 we awoke to a white world ... it was snowing again! We all hustled down to the field to drive the mother cows with their new calves into an empty hayshed. It had high walls and a good roof, so it was an ideal shelter for the twenty young calves and their mothers until the snow melted. We fed them in there, but we let the cows out to go to the river to drink in the morning.

## A CHANCE MEETING AT THE BUTLER DANCE

During the spring of 1941 I started to notice a change in my relationship with Issy. It had a lot to do with her new boyfriend, Ben Wilson, a local cowboy who had a reputation of being very good with horses. He worked for the Graham ranch with Alex Graham, and they had a big herd of horses that usually rustled the swamp meadows all winter. Ben would ride out on weekends to visit with us, but I knew it was just to see Issy.

There wasn't much time for visiting when all the ranchers were calving, which is why the Butlers always held their big spring dance after the cattle branding and turnout was done on May 15.

Branding time was serious business: every calf had to be branded with hot irons, and also marked to prove ownership. KB's mark was to crop the tip off the right ear and under slope the left ear.

At the same time that this was happening, the bull calves were all changed into steers by castration.

By May, Issy and I had the range cattle happily out on grass with salt, the calves were all branded, the garden was planted and the hayfields were being irrigated by Bev and KB.

We decided to attend the Butler Dance on June 1, leaving the men behind. We got our saddle horses in so we could leave early the next morning. Our dancing dresses and shoes were wrapped and tied behind the cantles of our saddles. Issy was excited because she knew Ben would be there too.

The spring morning was fresh with dew as we began our thirty-mile ride after we and the horses had breakfasted. By the time we were about three miles from the Butler ranch, the sun was hot and we were dusty.

The valley has several small lakes, and Issy led us down a side trail to one where we stripped off our saddles, hung our clothes on the bushes and refreshed ourselves. Our horses enjoyed the clear, cool water of this calm and private lake too, and came out glossy and rejuvenated. The warm sun and a light breeze dried us off.

We arrived at the Butlers' within the hour, so fresh that no one could believe we had ridden thirty miles that hot day. After our horses were unsaddled and pastured, we changed into our dancing clothes and had a grand time visiting, eating delicious food and then dancing all night. This was our pre-haying and fall round-up party, to last us until the cattle sales were over in October, which was four months away. The Butlers were very generous and hospitable, as they had been the year before when I attended; they shared their big living room, their communal saddle-horse pasture and all their food.

By 10:00 a.m. the party was over and folks were leaving. Issy told me she wanted my horse for Ben to ride with her to Tatla Lake. She said I could ride with the Graham family, as they had a vehicle. She would meet up with me at the Tatla Lake ranch about thirteen miles away.

I didn't mind, so I climbed into the dark, windowless, enclosed back end of the vehicle and sat on a bench along with the Graham ranch workmen. Some of them had drunk too much wine, and they were soon asleep on the floor and snoring loudly. The air was stale with sweat and alcohol fumes, and I was afraid I would throw up from motion sickness and the stench.

The only way to avoid it was to sing. A young fellow, nineteen or so, stayed up with me, and we talked and sang the whole thirteen miles. Finally the driver arrived at the ranch and opened the metal doors and let us out. That fresh air was a lifesaver.

All of the others went off to their Sunday beds, but I had to wait for Issy and my horse. I was so thankful to have staved off my nausea and to be back in the fresh air and sunshine. I went down to the edge of a small lake close by to rest and commune with the ducks. The young fellow I had been talking to came down to the lakeshore.

There was a rowboat pulled up onto the shore with oars in it. We pushed it out and climbed aboard for something to do, but the sun became very hot, so we parked it in the shade of some willows where it was cool and tranquil after the bedlam of the past night.

I asked him where he was from. "Alberta," he said. I told him I was from there too. He said he had heard good things about British Columbia, so he came job hunting.

"What did your folks say when you told them you were leaving?" I asked.

"Oh, my mom cried and my dad thought I should wait a while longer."

"Have you written home to tell them you're okay?" I asked.

"Naw, I don't write much."

"Well, guess what ... I love to write, and I carry paper and a pen with me to record stuff for the *Williams Lake Tribune* newspaper. So you tell me what you want to say to your folks and I will write it for you. That will be our good deed for the day."

He agreed, and I started off:

Dear Mom and Dad,

I'm a friend of your son, writing this letter as he dictates it. He is okay, just doesn't like writing ...

He went on to tell me about his job at the Grahams' ranch, how beautiful the country was and how friendly the people were while I wrote it just the way he said it. He talked about the dance and how most people came by horseback, and he raved about the Coast Range mountains.

I covered two pages and then we heard "Gerrreee!" and I knew Issy had arrived. I made him promise he would mail the letter and then I stepped out of the boat to join Issy with the horses. We said our goodbyes and I wished him well. I never did see him again.

## CROSSING CHILKO RIVER

Next on the list after our spring chores was taking Dolly's horses back to Minto. Issy and I set off on the journey once again. On the journey home, Ben met us so he could see Issy when we arrived at Chilko River.

There was no bridge over the river; only a cable crossing with a tower on each bank to anchor the connecting cable and a four-foot-square carriage on pulleys that people sat in while they pulled it back and forth by hand using a five-limb to hook the cable with.

But when we got there, the carriage was across on the other bank, which meant one of us would have to go get it. The river was high and dangerous, and I did not hear anyone offer, so I volunteered.

The Chilko River was turbulent with whitecaps and I couldn't swim. There's a saying: "When ignorance is bliss, 'tis folly to be wise." I just thought to myself, "What an adventure!"

I took my halter rope to sit in and found some cardboard to pad it with. I knew the cable could fray the rope while I was suspended, so I looked around and found a length of haywire. I wrapped it loosely several times around the cable and twisted the ends together to make a sturdy wire loop around the cable to feed my halter rope through twice.

When I was mounted up and dangling, I had Issy take my picture with my Brownie camera.

It was easy going down to the middle of the cable over the river, but all uphill from there. I stopped once to look down at the river ... that was a bad idea! It was rolling along so swiftly it was mesmerizing and I almost let go and joined it! I quickly focused on the waiting carriage while straining to pull myself uphill on the cable.

The carriage was tied to the tower when I got to the other side. I climbed aboard and rested, taking deep breaths. No one was clapping or cheering from the east bank like I thought they should be, though. Instead they were cuddling and kissing.

I hauled that carriage back across the forked hook and Ben grabbed it and tied it to the tower. I climbed out and rested while they unsaddled our horses and piled the rigging nearby to load into the carriage after they hazed the horses into the river.

I watched those brave horses wade out to cross. The current caught them and took them downriver, with only their heads visible. Then they were around the bend and out of sight.

I was worried and I asked Ben if they would drown. "Naw," he said, "they're all good swimmers. They'll crawl out and meet us on the other side."

When the rigging was loaded into the carriage, we climbed in and Ben powered us across the Chilko River. Sure enough, the horses met us on the other side, totally soaked. We waited until they dried off a bit, then rubbed them down with grass before we re-saddled them and continued on toward home.

## SEPTEMBER MOOSE HUNTING

KB had been big-game guiding and outfitting for about twenty years by the fall of 1941. Since he was herding his saleable cattle to market around September 15, he was able to book a couple of hunts beforehand, starting with the opening of the season on September 1. The bull moose go into their rutting stage in September, and it's hard to know what date exactly, as it depends on the weather. But the earlier the hunt, the better, if you want choice moose meat.

His first hunters, a party of two men, arrived by suppertime on August 31 to begin their moose hunt the next day. KB had licensed me as his assistant, which meant I was expected to go along. Bev wanted to come too, and Issy would stay behind to milk the cows and feed the chickens at home. We saddled five pack horses, taking one extra horse to carry our camp gear and pack the moose back to the ranch.

We rode up to a pass between two mountain ranges where there were two small lakes and swampy, willowy meadows—ideal moose pasture. We pitched our camp away from the lakes to not disturb the moose, staked some horses on a patch of good grass and hobbled the rest to graze. Our horses were used to the routine: we would switch them around before dark so every horse would get enough to eat.

We had a small campfire for coffee, reheated prebaked potatoes and prefried chicken and had garden salad. We had "hobo cake" for dessert, a fruit and nut cake baked in cans at home. To serve, we cut the bottom of the can fully around and pushed the cake out with the tin end. We kept the camp noise down, as sound travels clearly at night and we didn't want to alert the wildlife.

Next morning we were up at daylight, had coffee from a Thermos and set off to check out the meadows and lakes. KB and Bev took one hunter to the furthest meadow, and the other hunter and I stopped off at the first meadow. This way between all of us we had the pass covered.

KB must have heard a moose grunt, and he answered once and then waited very quietly. Five minutes later the bull noiselessly appeared looking for the bull he'd heard to challenge him. Kaboom! There was only the one shot. My hunter and I stayed quiet and listened.

When no more shots were fired, we snuck over to have a look. KB and his hunter had their knives out, ready to open the bull and bleed it. They wouldn't cut the throat if it was to be a mounted head.

"How come one shot killed such a big animal?" I asked KB.

"Well," he said, "Bob here did just what I suggested: if the bull presents himself head-end on, as he did, just wait until he turns his head and moves that big nose off to the side, giving you a clear shot at the chest. Be sure to hit the chest dead centre and he'll drop in his tracks."

I filed that tip away for future use. My hunter, who had been picking his way slowly up to where we were standing, moved in to eyeball the bull moose. "Whoo-ee!" he exclaimed. "It's the size of a horse."

Bob grinned at his partner.

"I don't think our car can carry two of them," my hunter said. "Do you have anything smaller out here?"

KB smiled. "Do you have a black bear tag?"

"I think I do. Why?"

"There could be a black bear on this gut pile by tomorrow, and a bear wouldn't be so heavy because you only take the hide and the two hams. They're very tasty."

"I'd be okay with that," replied my hunter.

We butchered out the moose and hung the quarters in the shade to cool out, and we went back to camp to have breakfast and switch the staked horses around onto fresh grazing.

We came back in a couple of hours with three pack horses to pack every part except the feet back to camp. The men lodged a strong, long pole between two very shady trees up high for the moose meat to be hung safe from predators overnight.

That evening we snuck back to see if a bear was there yet. No bear yet, but there were lots of crows.

The next morning before sun-up my hunter and I went to check again and sure enough, a shiny black bear was gorging himself on the guts in the cool of the morning. I had explained to my hunter that a spine shot just behind the shoulders would be best to guarantee that he shot the bear.

He leaned on a shady tree, took careful aim at the bear standing broadside and squeezed off the shot. The bear collapsed on the spot. I finished him off with my little 30-30 rifle with a heart shot, as my rifle made a smaller hole. My hunter produced a camera and I took pictures. We had the bear half-skinned before the rest of our crew arrived after they'd had their breakfast. I left the head and feet on the hide to be skinned out later. The men carried the two hams and the hide back to camp in the bright September morning.

We had lunch and then packed everything on our pack horses. The moose meat had cooled well overnight. We rode back home and those happy hunters left early the next morning.

## CHRISTMAS AND A STRANGE PROPOSAL

It was almost Christmas and Issy and I had a lot of fun preparing the ranch. I baked fruitcakes, killed and dressed the young roosters we had raised and saved deer ribs to make into spicy spare ribs, a delicious specialty. We hung popcorn strings and paper chains on the tree as we had no power for strings of lights. For light in those days we used a gas lantern over the table and kerosene stand lamps for the bedrooms. Candles were a no-no, as they were too dangerous.

All of us were home for Christmas dinner. Issy's boyfriend, Ben, came as well as all the other folks who happened to drop in. Our gifts were wrapped in brown paper and newspaper under the tree, and we made pull toffee and popcorn balls while the radio blared Christmas carols and down-home stories.

But when the news broadcast came on it was pretty grim. It seemed as though the Second World War was festering. We talked about what that might mean, but at that point we didn't think it might directly involve any of us. We carried on with our festivities as happily as we could.

One day in January, while Bev took his turn at feeding the herd at the meadow, KB took me aside. I was ironing shirts beside the cookstove, where I could keep the irons hot. I had just put one cooled-down iron back on the stove and clamped the iron handle onto a hot one. As I turned to my ironing board to finish ironing the shirt, KB sat in his rocking chair and said, "I wish you'd marry Beverly."

I almost dropped the iron on my foot! I was at a total loss for words. Outside of the kidding around and fun times that Bev, Issy and I indulged in, our camaraderie had no romantic overtures.

But here I was, faced with a suggestion—no, a *wish* from a man that I greatly respected. Could I trust his judgment? Bev was only nineteen at that point and still immature in my mind. But could he mature into the image of his father? KB hadn't even raised him.

I felt like perhaps I needed to be realistic, though. I tried to see though KB's eyes: the war was on and young men like Bev were being conscripted. It could happen, and he was KB's only son. KB probably wanted to see him married in case Bev ended up going overseas. And here I was, the same age, in love with this ranching lifestyle, competent and hard working. These were prerequisites for any Chilcotin wife, so I could see why KB was suggesting the union. The problem was, I had never considered being married until I was at least twenty-four.

With all these thoughts running through my head, it was no wonder I couldn't think of a thing to say. We left the conversation unresolved for the time being.

But soon one of KB's children would be married. By that time Ben and Issy were becoming quite serious about each other. Shortly after Christmas they announced that they were planning a June wedding, and none of us were surprised. I was happy for them, but sad that this meant Issy would be leaving the ranch.

Issy and Ben had started cleaning and painting their future home, a small house and property they rented just up the valley. It was for sale for one thousand dollars and KB had offered to purchase it for them but Issy, ever independent, was adamant that she and Ben pay for it themselves.

We were busy feeding cattle, branding calves and putting the cattle on the range, and the wedding was planned for after the work was done. Unfortunately, KB, Bev and I would have to miss the wedding in Vancouver as we would be putting out the bulls along with our other chores and we just couldn't take the time off to make the trip.

Ben and Issy would come right back after the wedding and settle in to their new home up the road and get to work. Ben owned a few head of horses and some cattle to bring to their small range and he planned to put up some hay. They would be living close enough to carry on helping us at the Circle X too, so I knew I would still get to see Issy from time to time.

## PREPARING FOR A JUNE WEDDING

With Issy and Ben's wedding looming only a month away, Issy and I were trying to get as much done as we could. We concentrated on spring cleaning the Circle X Ranch house. We hung all the blankets out on the clotheslines, washed the windows inside and out, put the woollen Stanfield's underwear away in mothballs and stored the lined winter boots up on a high shelf.

While we worked and talked about the big day coming ever closer, Issy didn't appear to be nervous. She was actually very matter-of-fact about it all. She had a plan for her life and it was about to be realized. Her future husband was a tall, handsome cowboy who could rope and break wild horses and do any kind of work that a ranch required. He was very good with a rifle, so they would always have meat in their larder, and Issy knew all about gardening so they were a perfect match for starting a home together.

I was happy for her, and told her so, even though I would miss her and I would have a lot more work to do once she was gone.

KB had mixed emotions with regard to the wedding. He was a typical father, so that meant no man was good enough for his daughter! He had enjoyed having his daughter back in his life, and in some ways he felt he was losing her again.

I wanted to lighten his gloomy mood, so I told him, "KB, look at it this way. You haven't lost a daughter, you've gained a son!"

That brought a wry smile to his face. "And how about you, Gerry?" he said. "You two have been like sisters should be. How do you feel?"

"Well," I said, "I figure they are not really leaving you—or me. They'll be living just up the road, so we'll still be a family."

That seemed to cheer him up.

Issy and Ben had their Vancouver wedding and moved into their new home to start their new life, and life at the Circle X carried on.


## THE RUNAWAYS

Soon it was haying season, and KB used his faithful, steady team, Roanie and Blackoby, for the dangerous job of mowing. He had prepared the haying equipment while Issy and I were trailing the horses to Minto earlier in June. He greased the wheel bearings of the mower and rake, and he sharpened two sickle blades for the mower while sitting on a bicycle seat attached to the metal frame that held the heavy stone. He foot-peddled to spin the big grindstone toward him to engage with the sections (teeth) of the mower blades to sharpen them. A tomato can, suspended above the grindstone, dripped water onto it to ensure a smooth grinding of the sickle sections. That job required concentration, and he held the five-foot mower blade up to the spinning grindstone with great delicacy.

By July he was ready to start mowing. After a couple of sunny days with light breezes, the hay was ready to rake into windrows, which was my job now that Issy was gone.

KB was mowing another field, and I was given a team of geldings, Pasco and Lightning. Lightning was given his name because he was so slow. He was part draft workhorse. I harnessed them both and drove them down into the field to hitch them to the hay rake.

All was going well as we raked the hay into windrows. I liked this team. They stepped out smartly, and I thought I could have that whole field raked by suppertime. But I would soon be proven wrong ...

The irrigation ditch bisected the field we were working on. It was a foot deep and about fourteen inches wide and dry. The way to cross it was to angle one rake wheel into it carefully, then go up and out while the other wheel angled in.

My team had been waiting for this manoeuvre ... and just as the first wheel came out, they bolted! The second wheel hit the ditch too fast, and I was almost thrown off. My seat cushion sailed away, the wrenches and tools in the tool can nailed to the tongue were pitched out and we were into a full-speed runaway.

I had the rake teeth-up and locked to cross the ditch. Now I dropped them to create drag. KB had told me, "If you're ever in a runaway, rein them into a circle." I tried, but Pasco was inclined to lie on the tongue, which I could see was cracked. I visualized it breaking and sticking into the ground, which, at their speed, would pitch the rake over their heads and dump me under their feet. I had to straighten them out and ride it through. I had been see-sawing on the reins, but it was no use: the straight bits were changed by their jaw teeth.

We were heading fast toward a patch of stumps in a part of the field that was being cleared. The horses ran right into it and stumps were whizzing by alongside the wheels, any one of which, if caught by the centre frame, would have bent the rake into a U-shape.

But my guardian angels were with me. The clover in that stump patch was three feet high and lush, and the teeth caught the clover and pulled the horses to a stop. I climbed off the hay rake, still holding the reins, and lay on the ground to calm my heart with deep breaths.

As I lay there underneath the cloudless sky, I saw a thick plume of smoke on the ridge of Potato Mountain going straight up and I wondered what it was. I unhooked the horses and led them back to the barn. KB, Bev and I would lift the rake and roll it backwards onto the fields later.

When I asked KB about the smoke, he said, "The mule deer bucks bed down in the scrubs on the ridge during the heat of the day to catch the updrafts. Wherever a Native man shoots a buck, he burns a big clump of scrub so the women in camp know he got meat. They bring knives and horses to that spot to butcher the buck and pack it in to their camp."

Before I went back raking the next day, I modified that team's bridles. I found pieces of chain with links of about half an inch for chin straps and attached them, one to each bit. Now I would have control. If I pulled on the reins, the chains would bite into their jaws, and the harder I pulled, the more it would hurt.

The next day, I was starting on a new field, raking the perimeter of a little island of trees. The hay grew up the slope, so to rake the edge I guided the left wheel onto the uncut hay on the slope.

But little did I know there was a reason why that hay hadn't been cut: KB had avoided it because he was aware that there was a big boulder hiding in the bush hay. Unfortunately I did not know about it, nor could I see it.

My rake wheel went up onto the boulder, tilting the rake at a steep angle, and before I knew it the horses had leaped into a run-away once again. One tooth was missing from the rake, allowing a gap for my head and shoulders to poke through when I fell. Unfortunately my left leg got run over as I was pitched off headfirst. I did a half roll to save my head. As I was thrown off, I hung onto the reins and got the horses stopped as I was being raked along the ground.

I tied the team to the trees on the island and limped the five hundred yards to the ranch house, thankful I hadn't broken any bones. I was hurt pretty badly, though, and I could see the bruising patterns of the wheel: thick rims and welded spokes angled across my leg below the knee, fast becoming purple. Oh my! And I was home alone with no one to help me. This would have to be a case of "Gerry, heal thyself."

I had an idea. We had tall creamers for the milk from our cows, which we cooled in the creek to make the cream rise to the top. They were about twenty-five inches tall, with a tap at the bottom to drain off the milk. They didn't rust because they were made of galvanized metal.

I put cold water into one empty one, and warm water into the other. My plan was to immerse my leg in the cold water for maybe ten minutes, then dry it and immerse it in the warm water for ten minutes to get the blood moving so it wouldn't form clots.

I kept the kettle heating to maintain the temperature of the hot water on the wood-burning stove. When KB came back to the house, he was shocked to see me sitting there in that condition with my leg soaking in the cow creamers.

He sprang into action to help me out and he agreed that what I was doing was a good idea. He got colder water from the pump to improve the circulation. We had to weigh the severity of the situation because there was no nurse nearer than Alexis Creek, which was about ninety-five miles from us, and we had no car. We stayed at the ranch using my home treatment and I was blessed, because it worked. I live to tell the tale and I didn't lose my leg or die from a blood clot.

## A SUMMER OF COWBOYING

After two years of working at the Circle X Ranch, I was pretty familiar with the routine. I missed having Issy's company when I went out on the range to check the heifers with the salt blocks, but our dog Jeff came along to keep us company. With Issy gone I had a lot more to do, so I became very organized. On nice days I would ride the range, and in bad-weather days I stayed at home to do baking and other household chores.

A typical day would mean that after breakfast, once I had the house tidy, I would ride the three miles up the slopes of Skinner Mountain to check the cattle and then be back to make lunch for KB and Bev. By then I was used to my 30-30 rifle, and I had to use it often to protect the cows. Coyotes would work in pairs to separate a mother cow from her young calf, but if we could shoot one coyote then the other one would quit, as she knew she now had the full attention of the mother cow.

As the cattle moved south along the range between the lofty ramparts of Potato Mountain and the shoreline of turquoise blue Tatlayoko Lake—a range of about two miles wide by fifteen miles

My horse Gypsy wasn't as quiet as he looks. I made the mistake of riding him bareback (without a saddle) one day—he reared and knocked out all my front teeth.

long—I couldn't come home for lunch anymore and had to take a lunch for me and the dog.

For this longer ride I took a pack horse with two blocks of salt, which was usually one week's supply, and used it, along with Jeff's help, to move the herd south onto fresh grass. The salt kept them within a mile radius.

Later in the summer, Issy would come and join me when I stayed overnight at the range cabin we had built. She came to spend time with me and also for the sheer enjoyment of the scenery and the sound of the cattle bawling to their calves.

The autumn cattle drive to Williams Lake would be my responsibility that year, and I would be accompanied by a neighbour. This left the Moore men to gather strays off of the summer range and herd them to Skinner Meadow. I was glad KB and Bev could have those three weeks to spend time together. They still had a lot of catching up to do from the years they were apart. They also had the task of taking the garden vegetables in before the deer ate them.

It was a beautiful time for a cattle drive. The poplars and balm of Gilead had all turned golden by September, and mixed with the green conifers along Chilko River they produced a beautiful landscape under the blue sky.

I surely enjoyed the beauty of the Chilcotin, no matter what the season.

## BEAR-FAT DONUTS

The route I would be taking with the other cowboys who were helping for the cattle drive was the same one Issy and I had taken going across country for four days to connect with the Chilcotin Road to Williams Lake. It was a shortcut, and easy on the cattle's feet, as it was grassy sod and soil.

When we reached Rawhide Meadow and allowed the cattle to spread out to graze their evening meal, one of the cowboys shot a black bear. I was in camp starting to make supper when the bear was shot, and I bridled my horse Brutus and jumped on him bareback to go see the bear.

He was fat and shiny haired. I knew the value of bear fat, so I skinned him, leaving the thick, white fat on the hide, then folded the flesh sides together and threw the furry hide across my horse's shoulders. When he didn't mind that, I jumped on behind the hide to ride back to camp with the bear's front and back leg skins flopping around Brutus's front legs—not many horses would tolerate that!

Back at camp I dragged the bearskin down, unbridled Brutus and turned him loose to graze again.

I had a plan. We had brought a cast-iron Dutch oven with us, and I opened the hide fat-side up and cut chunks of bear fat off to render in the pot on the coals of the campfire. While the oil was separating from the fat tissues, I mixed up a batch of donut dough from my biscuit-making ingredients. I had brought a piece of table cover, called oilcloth, with me for biscuit making, and I used it for patting the dough flat. An emptied tomato can cut nice big round donuts.

But how to cut the hole? Then I thought of my flashlight; the body of it was just the right match for size. The fat was getting hot enough, so I lifted the fat fibres out, popped in a donut hole as a tester and, when the temperature was right, I carefully lowered two donuts into the fat. When they were golden brown I drained them on a brown paper bag.

I loved being out on the horse regardless of the weather.

Putting the lid on the pot so no sparks could get in, I raked fresh coals over to my end of the fire, set the pot back on, and proceeded browning more donuts. The fellows had come to the campfire for their late lunch, and I set out a bowl with sugar for them to roll the hot donuts in. There was only room in the pot for three donuts at a time. I kept cooking until everyone was satisfied, and then I had some myself. They said those were the best—and most unexpected—donuts they had ever eaten!

After this adventure, the rest of the cattle drive was pretty routine. We did well at the sale, partly because our cattle had nice glossy coats from ranging at a high altitude all summer. Also, walking ten miles a day for the drive had helped them lose their belly fat.

I had no interest in the Klondike Dance this year. I hadn't bothered to bring a dress, because it would be no fun without Issy. We headed back for home the next day, hoping the good weather would hold.

I was so thankful to reach home at last and share the news of the sale. KB, wise man that he was, knew I was suffering from campout fatigue. I stayed in the house for a week and did the cooking, baking cakes, pies and cookies to go with the hearty meals of meat and vegetables. Everyone else did the outside chores, and then they'd come into the kitchen saying, "Hi Cookie! Whatcha got to eat?" I was happy to be left with my housework and preparing the meals.

By late November the squirrel skins were prime, as were all the other fur-bearers. I was ready to go trapping again. If the weather was fair, the dog and I left for the day right after breakfast, once I had the dishes done. I only stayed home if it was snowing hard. My trapline savvy was becoming sharper: I even caught a cougar with a snare in the centre of a thicket with part of a deer's ribs!

KB had started to talk about buying the 160 acres next door, now that Bev was part of the business. He was starting to think about building a big new log ranch house and he and Bev discussed the subject while I just listened. They decided to hold off on any plans for the time being, as winter was coming on.

# THE MARRIAGE OF BEV AND GERRY

Despite having to adjust to our new life with Issy being gone, KB and Bev and I were still like a big, capable, happy family. We worked smoothly together, joking, goofing off and enjoying ourselves while we got the jobs done. But sometimes I still missed Issy's companionship and the camaraderie we had all shared before.

One wintry day, KB and Bev fed the stock early out at the meadow and in the home pastures. Bev volunteered to stay up at the meadow to feed them the next day to give his dad a break.

I had noticed Bev was becoming more attentive in little ways. At first I just put it down to the fact that he was his father's son; his father had that Old World charm and was a gracious host with impeccable manners. It was only logical that Bev inherit those traits too. But I hadn't forgotten KB's wish that I marry Beverly ...

The news about the war was increasingly worrisome for KB. Having been though the first war, KB knew that Beverly could be called up to fight any day. Bev and I had discussed the war and wondered how it would affect the ranch and the lives of the family.

Sure enough, KB's fears came true. Bev got a notice that he was to be conscripted and sent back east to Camp Borden for training. He was advised to get his affairs in order. Well, this threw our platonic relationship into high gear. I hadn't planned on marrying for at least another four years, but then I hadn't expected a war, either. Now here we were.

Bev and I on our wedding day. We were married in Vancouver, so Bev's relatives could attend. After the ceremony we took a stroll through the big city.

I told myself that Bev had good qualities, and it was true. He was six foot two inches, blue eyed, strong and handsome. With such a fine-mannered man as his father, I reasoned Bev would develop the same qualities given time. I would be twenty-one in July, and Bev and I were the same age, so we decided to get married.

My dowry was money from the six hundred squirrel pelts I had harvested at twenty-five cents apiece. We set a date when Bev's relatives, including his grandparents, could all come.

And in early April 1943, we were married in a little white church in Vancouver. KB was unable to attend because he couldn't leave the ranch, but his wish had finally come true.

After the wedding we all continued ranching together until Bev was sent to Camp Borden, and then it was just me and KB on our own.

## BIG NEWS ...

KB and I managed to get the hay harvested and then it was time to round up the cows for the beef drive to Williams Lake for the sale in early October. KB and I were going to be the cowboys this time.

But I was keeping a secret from him. By mid-September I had realized I was pregnant. I was excited, but I didn't want it to affect the drive and I felt fine—I wasn't suffering from morning sickness. So I just kept on working, riding out to gather in the cattle, separate the beef and keep doing the Circle X Ranch chores as usual.

The cattle drive went fine, and I didn't tell KB he was going to be a grandpa until the sale was over. I knew he would have stopped me from going. When I did tell him about the baby, he was very proud and happy. Issy and Ben were expecting also, so KB could see the Moore family line continuing on. His hard work and planning were bearing fruit, so to speak, from both of his offspring.

KB suggested I should go to Kamloops to stay with my mother-in-law, Dolly, but I become nauseated on buses, so I refused to go. Then he insisted that my sister, Mabel, come stay with me until the baby was born, which I figured would be in the spring. To that I agreed.

Life carried on as usual. Bev was still at Camp Borden and KB and I went on with the chores. Eventually winter blew in. There was a two-day snowfall in early January, and I loved walking in snowstorms, so I decided to hike a mile to the lake. I would go alone, as my sister was baking. My plan was to set a snare for a coyote. Also, a pack of wolves had killed a cow of ours, which had been grazing with a few others on a natural meadow at the shore of Tatlayoko Lake, so I made up six poison baits to put under the carcass. That way the birds wouldn't get them: only the wolves could move the cow.

I set the snare, lifting a fifty-pound log above my head. It would balance there until the coyote tripped the snare. The log would fall, jerking the coyote up to hang by the neck. That done, I put the six poison baits under the dead cow for the wolves (I would later find out I got four), and I walked home.

By the time I got back I was doubled over in an intense pain that kept coming and going. My worried sister came out to meet me and I told her I was in labour. We were delighted. The baby was coming!

There was just one problem. It was January, so the stage had quit running, and there were no snowploughs. We had only our team and sleigh to get me twenty-three miles out to Tatla Lake, where I was to meet with a doctor. A neighbour rode there on horseback to the only phone, a party line, relayed halfway to Williams Lake by Alexis Creek, to get a doctor for me. The doctor had to come with Bill Sharp, the village police officer in Williams Lake, by car, often shovelling through drifts along the 230 kilometres of Chilcotin Road.

When one of our team became exhausted from pulling the sleigh through eighteen inches of snow, KB borrowed a neighbour's horse. Our other horse, Blackoby, soldiered on. He won much praise from all of us. We arrived at sundown in Tatla Lake ahead of the doctor.

The hospitable Graham family put me into the master bedroom off the kitchen. I lapsed into sleep several times, finally aroused by much hustle and bustle when the doctor arrived. He was washing his hands at the bedroom sink. They had forgotten the rubber gloves. A washcloth was draped over my face and ether poured onto it. I zonked out.

A wild dream, all in technicolour, took over. It was about a long, colourful queue of people winding down a grassy hillside to a free-standing door in the valley. They were going through and disappearing. When I finally reached the door, just as my foot raised and I was about to step through, someone standing by my side said, "I want that one," and pulled me out to stand beside him. Then, zip! I was back on the hilltop to wind my way down with the others to the door again, where all went through but then disappeared from sight.

Again, I attempted to step through but was again physically pulled out of position with the words "I want that one." I stood alongside what seemed to be a tall man. Then the dream changed. Then I heard a baby cry.

I was awakened to see a light bulb spinning crazily overhead. As it slowed and steadied, I saw Dr. Mackenzie splinting my baby's leg. My son was delivered alive after our seventy-four hours

I went into labour in mid-winter and I had to travel twenty-three miles to Tatla Lake by horses and sleigh.

of hopeless labour. His right femur had to be broken midthigh to deliver him feet-first. It was a partial breech.

Hodgson's stage wasn't due to come through for two weeks. Within two days I developed a devastating fever with chills, which I fought with every fibre of my being. These were the days before antibiotics. I couldn't die now: I had a baby to care for. Every day my baby's splints worked down and had to be reset by the wonderful Graham family. Hodgson's stage finally arrived and took me into the Williams Lake Hospital. My baby was admitted, but not me.

Dr. Pump was the only resident doctor, but he was a good one. He rebroke my baby's leg, taped small square blocks onto the soles of his feet and screwed cup hooks into the blocks. Long strings were fastened to the hooks, with the other ends holding weights dangling off the end of the crib. The baby lay on his back with both feet up at a right angle to his body. In a month I would be allowed to take him home.

Hodgson's stage returned us to Tatla Lake, where our team, sleigh and driver awaited us. It was a long, cold twenty-three

By late spring Marty had fully recovered from his broken leg.

miles mostly in the dark on February 24, 1944. Within a mile of the ranch, we had to abandon the sleigh and my box of apples because the road was too icy for the horses. The teamster took them up onto brushy hillsides to find safe footing. I carried my baby, whom we had named Martin Kennon Beverly Moore for his grandfather, in the freezing dark over that icy road, praying that we would not fall. The lamp in the window was a halo of gold. Grandpa Moore was waiting up for us, and he lovingly accepted his grandson from my weary arms.

## GETTING THE JUMP ON DISASTER

It took a while for me to fully recover from the trauma of baby Martin's birth, but within a couple of months it was time to get back to work. By then it was springtime, and we were turning our horse herd out onto the range where they had up to six miles of horizontal mountainside to roam. They would often split up into several bunches to graze the intermittent open, grassy hillsides bordering the south side of Skinner Mountain.

We always kept a wrangle horse or two in the home pasture so we could ride out to hunt for the herd when we needed them. This early range was a mile from home, which was handy. My favourite wrangle horse was Joe, a pinto gelding caught as a two-year-old by local Native friends out of the wild bunch and sold to me for thirty dollars.

When Joe and I hunted horses I gave him a free rein; he would carry me up the slopes to where we'd find their tracks. Joe would sniff their tracks, which were sometimes a few days old, and was always moving in the direction they were going. If there was a breeze, we would stop on a natural open meadow facing the wind; he would sniff the air currents, then start off of his own volition in a direction of his choosing. Presto! Within ten minutes we would come onto a bunch of horses.

Sometimes they were our neighbour's horses, so I'd say, "No, Joe, they're not ours. We have to look further." I'd rein him aside, and he would go willingly, always circling into the wind to pick up the horse scent.

Sometimes we'd get lucky right away by hearing one of the bells we hung on our horses, but in those cases the herd might have split up so the half-dozen Joe located didn't contain the one or two I was specifically searching for. I'd rein him aside again and we'd continue on.

In early spring, between May 15 and June 15, our heifers were also on this range with their young calves at foot. I always carried my 30-30 rifle in case a bear or coyote was harassing the herd. Two coyotes would work together, one antagonizing the mother cow until she chased after that coyote, while the second one slipped in and grabbed the young calf.

When Joe found the little bunch of horses I was after, I would dismount, drop the reins and start talking to them. "Hi, boys," I would say. "I've got oats for you, come on, come and get your oats."

I would untie the halters and the little cloth bag of oats from the saddle. They would cluster together, eyeing me and that oat bag. I would walk up to the one I wanted, give him a mouthful and slip on the halter before they surrounded me. Locating the second one, if it was on the outskirts, I'd pour a cupful of oats onto the ground to keep the bunch occupied while I slipped over, bag held out in front, to catch the reluctant one.

There was one time I'll never forget. It was a day in early June, and Martin was five months old. Our home had become a warm and wonderful place with the arrival of the baby, and his grandfather was very fond of him. The feeling was mutual; Marty would burst into smiles and giggles at the sight of KB beaming over the crib that he had made, kicking the blankets off and prying himself up by his elbows to be picked up.

Now, having finished his bottle, Marty was fast asleep in his crib with Grandpa nearby doing his record keeping, which would take two or three hours. I took this opportunity to saddle Joe and ride up to check on our two-year-old heifers with their calves. It was only a short mile, and barring any problems, I would be back before Marty would awaken.

It was a lovely day. Joe and I passed through the Circle X gate, and in twenty minutes we were up on the lush range of Sunflower

Hillside. The contrast of green grass and golden sunflowers was enchanting, given the added colour of the herd of red and white heifers grazing or lying there contentedly chewing their cuds while their month-old calves gambolled about.

The heifers were fine. Several of our horses were grazing nearby, so I caught up to two of them, putting on the halters I had brought in case I found them. We started for home on a cow trail through some brush that opened onto another parklike hillside.

About halfway in I saw a black bear only yards from the heifers. That was too close. Those new calves would be no match for a bear, nor would their two-year-old mothers know how to defend their first calves from such a predator.

I wrapped the two halter ropes around the saddle horn to take careful aim at the standing bear. I didn't normally shoot on horseback, although our saddle horses were all used to rifles being fired nearby.

It was too brushy to dismount to shoot, and since I was shooting at a right angle from Joe's left side I knew it would be okay. The horses were not aware of the bear, as he was uphill in some brush, and we were not upwind from him.

At that distance, about fifty yards, I knew I could drop him where he stood with one clean shot.

I pulled out my 30-30 and shot the bear. But instead of falling on the spot, he kept coming at full speed downhill and passed right behind the two horses I was leading! They panicked and bolted, one to each side of me. With the reins in my left hand and my rifle in my right, there was no time to unwrap the crisscrossed halter ropes. By now they were tightened on the saddle-horn and around my waist. I was in trouble.

My only chance to avoid a pileup was to outrace those two horses, which were now along both sides of my horse. I lifted the reins and dug my spurless heels into Joe's ribs. Being the excellent cow pony that he was, he leaped forward into a full gallop, took the lead and kept it by only half a horse length.

In two leaps we cleared the brush, bursting out into open space among big, scattered fir timber. The whole episode, starting with my rifle shot, felt like it had taken only two seconds.

After galloping for a hundred yards, the horses' panic subsided once they knew there was no bear behind them. I now had them under control. With my rifle lying across my knees, I pulled back to get the ropes off the horn and untwisted from around my waist. I walked all three horses to a grove of sturdy poplars, dismounted and tied them each to a separate tree.

Then, rifle in hand, I walked on shaky legs to a patch of grass where I sank gratefully down. I had expected the bear to drop dead, not turn toward me. I was in shock and still trembling from that unexpected turn of events. To relax my quivering body I took several slow, deep breaths. I was so thankful that Joe had outrun the other two horses, and glad that I had bought him that day instead of a more placid horse.

I lay there for fifteen minutes contemplating what could have happened with me lashed to the saddle horn. It would have been a three-horse pile-up, with serious injury to myself and all three horses. Whew!

I was over my shakes, so I picked up my rifle and walked back to see what had become of the bear. Maybe I had made a clear miss? Maybe the bullet had hit a tree behind him? I thought I had hit him but maybe I was wrong.

I soon discovered my instincts had been correct. I found him dead twenty feet below the trail, piled up in a heap from his mindless headlong charge off the ledge. My shot wasn't a crippling one, so he had obviously leaped into his preprogrammed descent until he dropped dead.

I returned to my horses, mounted my saddle horse, laid my rifle across my lap and headed home, leading the horses single file and fervently thanking my guardian angel ... I'd had quite enough excitement for one day, and I'm sure the horses had too.

## ANOTHER NEAR-DEATH ENCOUNTER

A couple of months after my bear encounter, Bev was finally allowed to come home on furlough in August 1944, much to our delight. It

Bev came home on furlough to see his first-born for the first time. He met up with us on the beef drive.

had been almost a year since we'd seen him and he would finally get to see his first-born son, who was eight months old by then.

We were making hay at the ranch when he came back and had just cut a whole field of clover and timothy hay. It needed a day or so to dry in the sun before we could turn the heavy windrows over with the horse-drawn rake to dry the underside. KB, Bev and I all decided to go boating down the lake to pick raspberries for the day. We would take our dog and baby Marty with us and enjoy a picnic lunch on Tatlayoko Lake.

The lake was dead calm that day, which was fortunate because the boat motor had quit. I had my Brownie Hawkeye camera, and I took pictures of Bev and KB working on the motor, backed by the Niut Coast Mountain range to the west. Once they had the motor running again we continued on our way down to the south end of the fifteen-mile lake. We enjoyed our picnic lunch and then filled our pails with raspberries and started back home. After half an hour of slow boating we saw something swimming in the lake. Thinking it was a moose, we circled to get a better look.

It wasn't a moose. It was an immense grizzly bear.

The bear became very enraged when we intercepted his swim toward the west side of the lake. He began lunging toward the boat, bringing his head and shoulders above the water with every lunge, mouth agape. It seemed as though time stood still, as the boat was barely crawling and the motor threatened to stall at any moment. I was holding the baby in my arms, visualizing being thrown into the water on the bear's next lunge.

Our dog was barking, the baby was crying, I was screaming,

the bear was roaring and the motor was sputtering. The bear was growling his rage at us as he tried to move toward the boat. Grandpa had his 30-30 rifle pointed at the bear at a thirty-degree angle as the boat slowly crawled by. It was terrifying. I was fully expecting to be flipped into the lake and wondered how I would cope, swimming a mile to shore in the ice-cold water with a baby in my arms.

The boat slowly meandered forward past the bear, and it seemed like all might be well, although at any moment it could turn in the water and attack our rear end. But all of a sudden, within fifty yards of the bear the motor sputtered to a stop!

The bear treaded water for a moment or two, seeming to contemplate whether or not to swim up and attack the boat after all, while Bev frantically attempted to restart the motor. After a couple of minutes with all of us in shock, the stress was released when the boat motor started up again. It was then that I remembered my camera.

"Oh my gosh!" I exclaimed. "I never got a picture. Circle him again, please, but not so close up." It seemed crazy, but Bev agreed and we kept a safe distance so I could get the picture. The bear continued on to the lakeshore and we watched him get out. Even with his hair all plastered against his body he was as big as a horse. We watched until he disappeared into the timber, and then we turned the boat homeward. I wondered if this was the grizzly bear that was known locally as Big Foot.

Later, while conducting a spring grizzly hunt with a Washington client, I came upon signs of a massive grizzly bear. There was a pine tree clawed and chewed up over nine feet above the ground, and nearby was an eighteen-inch grizzly track. In the old-growth timber there were piles of bear dung with a diameter of four inches. Each pile would have filled a bucket.

I never heard any mention of anyone ever killing Big Foot. We figured that he had come up the Homathko River travelling from the Pacific Ocean and had obtained his large size from living on salmon there. When he hadn't been seen for several years they speculated that he had probably gone back to his salmon-fishing grounds at Bute Inlet.

## BEEF DRIVE WITH BABY MARTY

Bev had returned to Camp Borden in preparation to being sent out overseas, and it was time for Grandpa and me to ready our camp gear for the beef drive, which would start in two days. We would be taking baby Marty with us this year, which meant taking the wagon pulled by Grandpa's dependable team Roanie and Blackoby. Grandpa would drive while I herded the cattle along behind.

The wagon eliminated the need for the pack horse that Issy and I had taken years before and meant we had more luxuries like a tent and vegetables from our garden, and—oh yes—Marty's potty chair and baby bathtub, which he also slept in. We also shot a fat, dry doe and shared half of it with our neighbours before leaving next day, bringing the rest with us.

The cattle, who were used to being fed hay in the winter, followed the wagon because it contained loose hay for us to sleep on. I brought up the stragglers. Twenty days later we reached Williams Lake and rented a cabin at Mrs. Hendry's auto court. Weparked the

We couldn't leave baby Marty home when we went on the cattle drive, so we took him and all his baby supplies with us, including his bathtub which doubled as his crib. He was a healthy, sturdy boy.

wagon out in front so its box could serve as a comfy bed for Marty's naptime.

We were excited when Bev arrived on furlough again, just in time for part of the drive. Just when he was supposed to leave on the ship overseas he was diagnosed with rubeola (red measles), so his ship left without him. I guess he just wasn't destined to go to war. It would be a short visit with us and he would be returning to Camp Borden soon.

As usual, the town put on a big dinner for the ranchers, and since KB had won a silver loving cup for the ten best yearling steers, we got to sit at the head table. KB hadn't been to a sale for a few years so he was happy to visit with the other ranchers.

When we had paid all our bills, we loaded our wagon with supplies for the winter: cases of tomatoes, dried prunes, apples and pears, sacks of flour and sugar, chicken feed and oats for the horses.

We arrived back home a week later and we found that our garden had been eaten by deer. The broad beans were just two rows of stalks, the peas were totally gone, the carrots had all their tops chewed off and the turnips were like a row of bald heads with tooth marks. They were the only survivors.

We moved the cattle up to the meadow to rustle and the ranch hummed along while we battened down the hatches for winter.

Before Bev left again, Grandpa asked us if we should build a new log house with running water. We thought it would be a good idea to make a floor plan and save up for concrete for the full-sized basement we wanted. Issy, Ben and their kids would share it with us, and we were all excited. It was KB's dream house. We decided that KB and I would fall trees and peel them next spring, then deck them and cover them to cure in readiness for house building.

# MAKE WAY FOR BABY #2!

Despite our big plans, the house building needed to be put on hold, because it turned out I was pregnant again. The following June I gave birth to my second son, Barry Graeme Moore, a chubby ten-pound baby with curly, reddish brown hair.

My mother had come to help with Marty and insisted that I go to the Alexis Creek outpost hospital to have the baby or she wouldn't stay. I agreed to go and I ended up being there for five weeks. Barry had just been born when Bev, who had been home on leave for two weeks, roared up under the window on his motorcycle at 7:30 at night. He got to meet his son right away, but it would be a short visit; he had to return to Camp Borden immediately after. During the war years our lives were quite disrupted. There were no set dates when Bev would be home, and of course we had no telephones, and mail was twice a month. So he just showed up every so often for a couple of weeks.

There was talk that the war would soon be over, but everything was so uncertain. I was glad to have him come home on leave and it was too bad he had to leave so soon after the baby was born. We would just have to wait until Bev was formally discharged before life got back to normal.

Meanwhile, the nice women at Alexis Creek came a couple of days later to my bedside to hold a baby shower, and I was thrilled. I had not had one when Marty was born, so this was a pleasant surprise for me.

I had two young boys by the time I was twenty-four. Marty is two years old and Barry is less then nine months old.

They gave me many thoughtful gifts like handmade knitted booties, a crocheted blanket, cloth diapers hemmed to different sizes to use as the baby grew—and a bottle of perfumed lotion for me! It was such a nice thing they did, and I sure appreciated it.

Grandpa Moore was delighted when the Andersons brought me home and I handed over his second grandson, who was a robust little fellow. I had not been able to nurse Marty after he was confined to the hospital. I was so ill in the two weeks after his birth that it was better for him to be put on formula. But with Barry, nursing was routine.

## Baby Barry and the Bunch-Quitter Bull

By mid-July Bev was home again, so he and I would ride down range to check on our cattle. I took six-week-old Barry with me on my saddle horse. I put him on a pillow in front of me with a broad scarf tied around us both.

One time we found the herd had drifted further south, parallel to the end of Potato Mountain. They were all fine, present and accounted for, except for our prize bull, a well-built three-year-old registered Hereford. We searched the area and counted our animals, but he was the only one missing.

Our neighbour's summer range was up on Potato Mountain. We checked the drift fence, which was a stout log fence between our range and his, there to prevent the herds from mixing. The tracks left by his cattle and saddle horses were two days old going through the gate. That gave us a pretty good idea of where our bull was.

We were tired, as were our horses, but the only thing to do was go up the mountain, find our bull and bring him back to his own herd. We camped overnight so we could get an early start. In the morning we rode up seven miles and located the neighbour's cattle near his salt trough, and sure enough, there was our bull, holding forth as though he was king of the herd.

We needed to rest our horses for an hour before tackling the job of separating him to bring him back. We unsaddled so the horses could roll before grazing the lush mountain forage. While they did that with hobbles on to keep them nearby, Bev and the baby and I had our brunch and relaxed. I had nursed Barry earlier, so he was sleeping peacefully.

By the time Bev went to collect our horses it was going on to four o'clock. We wanted to get our bull back with his herd before dark so we could still have daylight back at our camp to prepare for the night.

We saddled up to get at the job with baby Barry cushioned in his special spot, tied to me with the scarf on the front of my saddle. We cut the bull out along with three cows for company and started them back down the trail. I rode the trail and Bev and our heeler collie rode the sides through the timber to discourage the cows and bull from turning back.

It would be a couple of miles of mountainside before we reached the level bottom trail. The drift fence was still four miles away. It was lucky that Bev was riding a good timber horse, as the animals were determined to break back and away from the trail and return to their herd. Whenever Bev got them back onto the trail we chased them along quickly when they left the trail. Mikey the dog heeled them back on out of the bordering forest. He was worth six cowboys.

When we reached level going we allowed the cows to drop off. But the bull refused to proceed without them, so Bev roped him by the horns and tied him to a stout, green pine that would hold him overnight, and we rode five miles back to our camp. We watered all four horses (our two pack horses were staked at camp) and restaked them all on fresh grass, made a fire, had a quick meal and went to bed, satisfied that our bull was short-anchored for the night. We'd deal with him again come morning.

A rosy dawn broke, the birds tuned up and we shared our chores. Bev watered and restaked the horses while I warmed a basin of water to bathe Barry before starting breakfast. He was a real trouper, this baby boy: only six weeks old, and already herding cattle! After I fed and changed him, I left him to roll and kick on a blanket until we were saddled up and ready to ride.

Coffee, fried eggs, bacon and toast never tasted so good! After restaking our pack horses and hanging our food from a high, horizontal pole away from bears, we all rode off again to engage with our bunch-quitter bull.

He was standing quietly beside his tree, but we could tell by the torn-up ground all around him that he'd had a busy night. We decided we would try leading him instead of driving him. Bev untied the rope from the tree and climbed back onto his big gelding. Bev pulled hard on the rope at a right angle from the bull.

The bull swung around and Bev moved ahead to the trail with the bull following docilely along. I brought up the rear behind the dog, who took his place right behind the bull. We went through the drift fence, closed and braced the gate and continued on about a mile to the salt blocks we had packed in by horseback for our herd. There were about thirty head of our cattle, plus one of our two-year-old bulls, at the salt.

Bev rode up beside a tree to wrap the rope around to hold the bull until he could dismount and release him. With the tree between himself and the bull, Bev gave a little tug on the rope and the bull stepped forward, allowing enough slack for Bev to slip the noose off over his horns.

Amazingly, the bull was halter-broke! The breeder that KB had bought him from must have taught him to lead as a youngster, and he hadn't yet forgotten it. But it took a stout tree and a long night to remind him.

While we fixed some lunch to eat before packing up to return home, our prize bull reintroduced himself to the few present females, totally ignoring the young bull; he was still the king.

After lunch we rode off toward home, mission accomplished.

## GRANDPA'S SAWMILL

With the ranch work going well and the kids growing fast, Grandpa Moore started planning his dream again: that big log ranch house he wanted so badly. He had already drawn up the floor plans, and when Bev had been on leave over the past year or so, he had helped skid out some fir logs for the walls.

KB knew he needed a good power source to run a sawmill, cut the lumber and build parts of the inside, like the walls, floors and stairs.

He found an ad for a Yellow-Knight bus motor with plenty of horsepower. The only problem was that it was down near Vancouver. But such was his determination that he enlisted Bev and me to go down, check it out and hopefully buy it. We would also need a truck big enough to haul it.

"But what about the kids?" I said. By then Marty was three. Barry was only twenty-three months old and he was a very active child. I wanted to take the trip, but I knew they were a handful.

"Don't worry," said Grandpa, "I'll watch them. We'll be just fine; just go get us a motor for the mill."

So off we went. Bev and I took the Greyhound bus down, checked out the bus motor, and found an old truck that was big enough and within our budget. We left Vancouver in high spirits. The weather was fine, and we had the bus motor chained down and the wheels chock-blocked on the flat deck. The truck had no

Grandpa (KB) was living his dream of building a beautiful ranch house, but first he had to get the sawmill working. Here the crew takes a break after running logs through the new mill to make boards for the house.

cab, which was why it was cheap, and we did get some funny stares from other motorists seeing us sitting up on the seat with only the bulkhead at our backs.

Things went fine until we came to hilly country, where the motor would stall. It was hard to change to a lower gear and hello … we discovered it had no brakes! As soon as we were aware of that, we borrowed a couple of blocks from a handy wood pile on the outskirts of a small community.

When we heard and felt a stall coming on I jumped out, grabbed a block of wood and put it behind the back wheel until Bev could restart the motor, get into a lower gear and creep forward. Then I would grab my block, throw it up onto the floor, leap up to regain my exposed seat and hang on!

We managed to get to the 70 Mile stopping house by evening. We were very hungry and weary, so we had supper and stayed the night, thankful for the hospitable folk on this tiresome road.

The owner came out with us to check our weird truck and load. Bev told him about the motor conking out and the truck being hard to shift. The stopping house owner lifted the hood and chuckled: "There's some of your trouble right there," he said. "You've got a mouse nest on your motor." We hadn't even checked under the hood!

The man cleaned it off, Bev started the motor and it sounded much better. We thanked our host and left feeling a bit foolish.

The truck ran better after that, but it took us three slow days to get home. By the time we got back, KB was wondering what had happened to us. As I suspected, he had difficulties doing the irrigating and minding the boys during our long absence.

Bev and his dad soon had the irrigating caught up, and then they set up the motor beside the sawmill about one mile from home at a good stand of fir timber. The big engine had power to spare. Grandpa began sawing his log pile into lumber with help from Bev, as well as anyone else who could spare some time stacking lumber.

Bev and Grandpa rolled up a log at a time to be sawn into boards. It was an exciting experience, with the noise, the fresh sawdust smell and the cheerful conversation while the motor idled as they stacked bright, new boards or got another log on the ramp.

Issy would bring her two little girls to play with our two little boys and she helped pile lumber while I watched over the kids, prepared lunch on a campfire and made coffee. It was a great family effort, which inspired peace and happiness with Grandpa at the helm and everyone eager to help. To save fuel for the sawmill, we used the team and wagon and hauled our boards home to stack in the shade until they were needed.

## A CHRISTMAS CALF

That winter Bev was away at Camp Borden and KB and I had been taking turns watching the kids and rounding up stray cattle for weeks, searching the range through November into December and wishing for snow for easier tracking. Three days before Christmas, Grandpa came in stomping fresh snow from his boots and said, "A mother cow is missing from the herd!"

I had a stout saddle horse, so I volunteered to go down range and hunt for the missing cow. Grandpa had our calf herd to feed that morning, so he would take the boys on the sleigh, pulled by Roanie and Blackoby. He suggested a likely place to look. "Better take a lunch," he advised. "It's a twelve-mile ride one way. And be back by dark, eh?"

I dropped my lunch into the saddlebag, whistled up the purebred Airedale terrier a friend had loaned to me, mounted my horse and rode off.

It was a fair day, cool and crisp, with four inches of fresh snow muffling the sounds of my horse's hooves. We had made good time at a fast walk for about ten miles when I stopped to rest my horse and eat lunch. The snow was deeper this far down range, and I had seen no cattle tracks so far, so I'd have to go yet another two miles to get to where KB had specified.

Mounted again and moving on, we cut the fresh track of a large cougar. My first thought was that perhaps its tracks would lead me to the cow. I began following the track, which led uphill through big fir timber and along the rim of a deep creek canyon.

Glancing down into the canyon, I saw a mule deer lying dead some seventy-five yards below me. Crouched beside it was a big cat staring up at me.

I jumped off and tied my horse before alerting the dog. The movement spooked the cat. He lit out up the far side of the canyon in great leaps, clumps of small firs screening his body from view.

Without stopping to remove my chaps, I plunged down the steep incline, telling the dog to "go get 'im, boy!" until, sliding and jumping windfalls, we arrived at the deer carcass.

The dog was supposed to be a great cougar dog, and he huffed and snorted around the deer on the fresh scent, then struck off at a run up the slope on the cougar's tracks. I had a hard time following and grabbed onto the little firs, slipping and falling into the powdery fresh snow, but finally pulled myself up to the canyon rim.

There the dog's and the cougar's tracks struck off at a right angle to the rim. Any moment now I expected to hear the dog bark, which would mean the cougar was treed.

I ran as fast as my flapping chaps would permit for a half mile or so, which was not so easy as the snow was deeper out in the open away from the big firs. Then I heard the dog barking. It sounded like it was coming closer.

I waited, catching a much-needed breather.

Three deer came bounding into view—with the Airedale in full pursuit!

About then I was wishing for my rifle. For this crime, I'd have dropped the dog in his tracks. As it was, I yelled and scolded him loudly, whereupon he quit the deer and came skulking back.

The cougar would be long gone by now, so we returned by way of my tracks back into the deep canyon and up to my horse. Mounted again, we resumed the hunt for the mother cow.

A half hour later I came upon calf tracks in the foot-deep snow. Circling about, I found the little fellow poking his snow-encrusted face in under clumps of small trees to forage on the dead and dry grasses exposed there. He looked at me dazedly and went on nibbling the grass.

I circled some more, picking up his concentrated tracks, which led me to his dead mother's frozen, snow-covered body. He had been hanging around her—the only company he had in this wintery world.

He was lucky to have survived the cougar and coyotes so far. My pony was not a trained roping horse, so I'd have to use a little strategy here if I was to rope this calf without an energy-depleting chase.

I approached him quietly from the offside and carefully nudged him in the direction of his mother. When he was near her and I was ready with my loop, I gave out a cow bawl with a mama-like ring to it. He stopped and, with a hopeful little bleat, turned to face me.

I dropped my loop over his head.

Dallying the rope quickly on the saddle horn, I was ready when he bolted away: he snapped around as he hit the end of the rope, which dumped him in the snow.

I leaped off my horse and tied the loose end to a tree just as he was regaining his feet. Then I went along the rope with the intention of throwing him down to fashion a war bridle on him, so I could teach him to lead without strangling him.

We went around and around, tangling ourselves in the rope and among the bushes, but I finally threw him down and fixed the rope halter on his head. He was the dead heifer's first calf and weighed about eighty pounds.

He was pretty well tuckered, so while he was catching his wind I got onto my horse and, untying the rope from the tree, dallied it on the saddle horn. "Okay, little fellow, we're going home," I told him.

Coaxing my horse into a walk, we proceeded toward the cattle trail with the calf skidding on all four legs, his head just a-bobbing. Every few yards I'd stop to let him catch his breath or, if he was flat out in the snow, wait until he got up again. As soon as he was standing easy we'd go some more, each time with a little less resistance from him, until finally he was coming more willingly, if a little stiff-legged.

My back trail was the only broke track in all this snow, so I shooed him in front to see if he'd drive. He liked that idea, so we made better time then, though he was still going at his own pace.

The December daylight was fast disappearing and we were still a long way from home. Soon the stars came out and a cool north wind began to blow.

The frowzy little Hereford calf was now covered with frozen-on snow and was visibly tiring. There were six more miles to go, but he probably wouldn't make it. We had reached the log-branding corral down on our spring and fall range, so I herded the little fellow into it for the night. Breaking off an armload of fir boughs for him to munch on or lie on, I left him and rode on home in the cold starlit night.

Grandpa was saddling up to go hunt for me when I rode into the yard. It was 2:00 a.m.

"What happened to *you*?" he demanded, his voice heavy with concern.

"I found the cow dead, so I roped the calf to bring it home," I said.

"Well, where is it?"

"It got too late, and he was so all-in that I put the poor little fellow in the branding corral down range overnight."

"Well, I'm sure glad you're back," he said. "I was really worried." He took care of my horse so I could go on in and get warm. I didn't tell him until the next morning about chasing the cougar.

The next day I saddled up early and set off to bring my calf home. Christmas Day panic was setting in, as I still had a lot to get ready for the kids, but first things first. Especially when those things involved a little orphan calf stranded in the deep snow miles from any care and attention. No rancher could ignore that, no matter what.

When I reached the corral, the calf seemed almost glad to see me. He looked much better for his rest. The sun was high and it was a lovely day.

"Heck," I said to myself, "it's so early in the day, I'll just go spend a little time tracking that cougar before I start home with the calf."

So minded, I kicked my horse and set off down the trail to pick up the cougar's tracks, with the Airedale trotting willingly behind.

Some time later I picked up the big spoor and followed it

through the forest into broken, ridged-up country that was tough going for my horse.

The cougar track finally joined up with a whole herd of cat tracks. It seemed there were at least five in the pack. So engrossed was I in unravelling this twenty-four-hour story that I paid no attention to time, until whoops ... the sun dropped behind the mountain range, and I knew I'd best give it up.

Back to the cow trail we went, and we hustled along to the corral. The calf remembered what he'd learned the day before and willingly took the lead on the return trail, which by now was well broken. Night set in and the stars came out. The coyotes howled and trees popped in the frosty air as we plodded steadily homeward.

I was genuinely sorry to be worrying KB this way; I hoped that he would stay in bed tonight and leave me to my own hardship. The ranch house was dark when I arrived, and the yard was silent.

My calf was still covered with frozen-on snow. The only warm place to put him was the chicken house. A clutch of sleepy-headed chickens grumbled at the disturbance as the blast of wintery air entered along with the calf. I threw him an armful of green clover hay. Then, putting my horse away in the corral, also with a feed of hay, I stumbled to the house, stiff with the cold. Grandpa had gone to sleep this time.

By daylight I was up, none the worse for my experience but haunted by the realization that this was Christmas Eve and we were not ready because of my cougar-tracking adventures!

Grandpa, in his usual cheerful manner, told me what a surprise he'd had when he went to feed the chickens and found a bright-eyed and feisty little beasty, all dried off and right on the fight.

My sons named the calf Nicholas. And we all happily—though belatedly—set about with Christmas preparations now that the roundup was finally over.

## MAKING HAY AT SKINNER MEADOW

When the boys were young we rode together on my saddle horse when we went out to the meadows, Marty behind me and Barry tied with the scarf in front of me. As the boys grew bigger, I rigged two wooden packing boxes to sit on their horse, each with a low block of wood and a cushion for the boys to sit on. Their horse, which I led, was very gentle and dependable. By then Marty was three and a half, and Barry was twenty-six months.

In July a whole crew was making hay at Skinner Meadow and I was doing the chores at the ranch in the mornings and evenings. Bev was home to help with the haying.

I would feed everyone a huge breakfast, if they were home, and send them off with a lunch. Then I fed the chickens, milked the two cows and baked the bread. Sometimes the men stayed at the meadow cabin, in which case they made their own breakfast and I brought lunch up.

My little guys loved to help do the chores. When we were done they would sit in their packing boxes with containers of food at their feet, the heavier stuff in little Barry's box to balance the pack. Away we would go up to the meadow to have lunch with the crew.

We would all sit in the shade of a grove of trees on the edge

The whole crew would gather to help bring in the hay. I would cook a huge amount of food for breakfast and lunch so the hands could keep working.

of the meadow, where the men could lie about on the grass after stuffing themselves. The newly mown hay smelled so marvellous, the creek flowed fresh and cool and tidy haystacks loomed here and there on the big meadow.

My little Marty summed it up perfectly when he said, "Picnic every day, Mommy!" which brought a chuckle from his dad and grandpa and the rest of the crew.

In their free time, Grandpa and Bev would work on digging the basement for Grandpa's dream home. The war was over and soon Bev would be discharged from the army and home for good. Grandpa was looking forward to that, and so was I. He was hoping to get more done on the basement, so whenever there was a day here or there to let the hay dry or our mower man was cutting a new area, the Moore men would get to work. They dug the basement out of a steep slope. The horses pulled a Fresno, which hauled the soil to be dumped below the slope to create a level lawn for the walk-in basement.

The concrete for walls was mixed in and powered by wheelbarrow (a slow and tedious job) into the lumber forms. Grandpa had cut a lot of lumber on his sawmill for the forms. Soon ranch business called a halt, but at least we had the basement. We would get logs for the house the following spring.

I helped wherever I could. I would load the kids back into their boxes and mount my horse, and we would stop off at the meadow cabin to wash the dishes and tidy up the joint. I usually had food to leave for their supper: a roast, home-baked bread, quite often a pot of stew, which was the men's favourite, and snacking cookies.

Then we'd get back on our horses, boxes balanced with a stone or two, and walk the horses the six miles home in the late afternoon.

Transporting the crew in our motorboat. Barry is on the left, swaddled in blankets, and KB is sitting beside me on the right.

# BIG CHANGES AT THE RANCH

Bev finally recieved his disharge from the army in 1945 and returned for good after so many years of short visits. I was happy to have him back and be one big family again. We tried to pick up where we had left off, but he had changed somehow and it just wasn't the same.

Shortly after he got back, Ben and Issy separated and she left to move in with her mother, Dolly. Soon Bev got a hankering to go see how his mother and sister were doing. It was November, and I was loath to leave Grandpa with all the work when winter was coming on, even if it was only for a week. Grandpa had been ailing, but he refused to give in to it and go see a doctor.

"You go and see them," I suggested to my husband. "We can't both go and leave your dad. He's not well enough to do everything alone right now."

So Bev left. And he didn't return.

Shortly after, he wrote asking me for a divorce. I was shocked.

It was also upsetting for KB, because his wife had left him when the children were young. And now his son, married with two children, had done the same thing. He tried to think of something he could do to fix it. He told me he had contacted Bev to ask him to meet up in Williams Lake to tell him what he planned to do about his children.

When they met, at first Bev didn't really understand.

"They are your kids," KB explained. "You have to find a way to support them!"

They talked it out and Bev finally agreed that he would turn over his third share of the ranch to his kids for their support. Grandpa had the papers revised and signed. I was still trying to come to terms with what had happened, but I was glad to have KB looking out for the kids' best interest.

That winter was a time for both KB and me to take a step back to revisualize our lives. He had been so happy when Bev was finally released from the army and came home to stay, as was I. But we were still a family. Grandpa still had two little grandsons bearing his surname, and I was thankful that I was able to hold up my end and follow Grandpa's positivity.

He continued caring for the cattle up on the meadow and was coming down on weekends. We were too short-handed to manage everything with two toddlers to watch over as well, so Grandpa hired a nice live-in couple from Europe who had two children as well. This worked well for all of us. My kids now had company, and the parents were lovely people and a great help at everything.

The young man and I fed the calves and bulls with our team while the children were all safe indoors or out with his wife watching over them. She was an excellent cook too. When Grandpa relaxed at home on weekends, we checked the house plans for his dream house. Despite Bev's leaving, it was still going to be built.

## BECOMING A BIG GAME GUIDE

Life carried on without Bev, and I was busy starting to learn the guiding business from KB. Grandpa was a Class A guide, which permitted him to take hunting clients after whatever big game was in season. With spring bear hunting and fall moose, mule deer, and bear hunting, he needed an assistant guide. Grandpa said I should become a licensed guide because I could always see the game, so he bought an assistant's licence for me. It wasn't hard for me to learn to track, pack a horse and clean and skin an animal.

Whenever I could, I would leave the boys for the day and go along to learn the business. The road ended at our ranch and game animals were numerous, so we could just hunt out of the ranch

On our way home from a hunt we came upon this four-point deer. He was so beautiful that we left him to his business.

and return in the evening. Grandpa had apprenticed as a guide outfitter with Ralph Edwards of Lonesome Lake. Because I loved the wilderness and the adventure of stalking game animals, he figured I would be a natural. One day he asked, "So how about it? I want to quit." This began my fifty years as an A-Guide, outfitting and guiding hunters for moose, mountain goats, mule deer and black and grizzly bears that preyed on our cattle.

I always allowed two days between hunts to bake enough bread, cookies, etc., to take on my ten-day hunts as well as to supply Grandpa and the boys. As a guide outfitter I was responsible for advertising. Thinking I was on the right track, I put an expensive ad into *Outdoor Life* magazine and received a dozen letters from US hunters. The letters I typed and mailed listed animals available, dates, rates, maps and suggested clothing. I also stated that I was a woman guide outfitter. Bad idea. No one answered. From then on, letters returned to me were addressed "Dear Sir."

## BUILDING GRANDPA'S DREAM HOUSE

Spring can be a marvellous antidote to hard times, and this March was no exception. By now the cattle were all at the home ranch for calving time and we no longer had to divide our time between home chores and feeding the cattle at Skinner Meadow every day.

Grandpa and I took the boys with us for feeding and calving. They loved to ride on the hay slip behind the horses. They rolled up and played on the stacked hay while we pitched a load onto the hayrack, then the cows followed as we pitched it off to them. Grandpa and I took turns, one forking off the hay while the other kept the boys safe by letting them drive, each holding a rein. The new calves bounced around, butting heads, which delighted the boys even more.

In no time it seemed mid-May was smiling on us, and it was time to brand the calves and put the cattle out on the grassy range. I salted and moved the cattle and Grandpa began falling selected trees for his new ranch house. I avoided sorrowing over

After finishing our chores we all went berry picking down the lake. KB is on the far right. I am standing behind the rowboat, Barry and Marty are in the boat. We were joined that day by family friends.

KB's new ranch house.

my scuttled marriage; what would be the point? And anyway, we had a house to build.

The little boys, romping and tumbling about, followed their grandpa everywhere and made everyone's days happier. With the ranch to run, we had to consider any work toward building the house as our recreation time.

With the help of Roanie and Blackoby, Grandpa dragged in the logs near the foundation so we could peel them and leave them to dry and shrink a bit in the sun. Grandpa attended the irrigation as well in early May. He built a mitre box to fit the log ends, so they could be precisely sawed. This style was called Hudson Bay or pig-trough corners, he told me.

Burning KB's pioneer ranch, which was the first house built in the valley.

We used pulleys, cables and the team to roll the big fir logs up on log ramps to drop them into position with cant hooks. The walls were forty feet long by twenty-eight feet wide, but the south end was to be all windows with support posts between.

Grandpa's dream of a big family home was finally taking shape. The main floor was supported by huge log beams from underneath. This house was built to last. By the time the building was ready for the roof, a family had moved into the area, and Grandpa hired the husband to help him with that.

We had Christmas in the new house that year. No other family members came, and Grandpa was a bit disappointed because he had designed the house with a large front room that could accommodate local dances and other gatherings of the neighbours as well as his hunting guests.

In the full-size, walk-in basement, Grandpa built a seven-foot square concrete fireplace, steel lined. It was open on two sides for comfort and built in the middle of the room. The roof had no peak; instead it had a four-foot-wide flat walkway. Years later, my boys would climb an outside ladder and look over the field and hillsides at the deer browsing across the river in spring. They took blankets up there to relax on.

By 1950 the new ranch house had running water and a power plant provided lights. The windows were curtained, and comfortable couches and chairs were added. Grandpa and I threw a house party and neighbours came from near and far to congratulate KB on his handsome and sturdy new ranch house. We served roasts of beef, moose, deer and even cougar, each one tagged with its own name. Several neighbours had never had cougar, which is a white meat that tastes a lot like chicken.

Some folks brought their musical instruments to play songs people could dance to in the big sunny front room. We also had a record player with platter-style records that played yodeling Wilf Carter and bands popular at that time. Of course, those who made beet or dandelion wine brought some along.

It was a housewarming to remember, and Grandpa thoroughly enjoyed it.

## BREAKING TRAIL UP POTATO MOUNTAIN

There was one aspect of ranching that really bothered KB every spring: the sinister weed called milk vetch. If cattle, milking cows specifically, graze it when it's in bloom, they become addicted and will seek it out, ignoring regular range grasses. Soon their milk for the new calf dries up, and the cow develops a cough, loses weight and can die if it's not removed from the area.

The only remedy for us was to move the cows to Potato Mountain, which had alpine pastures where milk vetch didn't grow. Our nearest unoccupied meadow on Potato Mountain was at the north end. There was no trail to get there, or if there had been, it had grown in. Grandpa and I decided to plot a trail route. We took our binoculars to our south field, which provided an unrestricted view of that part of Tatlayoko Valley: a view of Potato Mountain to the east and the Niut Range to the west from an altitude of seven thousand feet.

We sat on the spring grass mapping it out, with Grandpa glassing the slopes while I sketched the terrain. The treetops ceased abruptly before a grassy ridge hugging the rocky mountainside. Grandpa handed me the binoculars. "Check out that open burned-off ridge," he said. "We could lay our trail on that. It's not too steep and it's all grass. Then we could swing north onto that little grassy bench above the fir trees growing out of that steep canyon. See what I mean?" He was his old pioneering self, excitement in his voice, a sparkle in his eyes.

"Yes, yes, I see it!" I said. "No sign of a creek from here. The ridge heading north to south up on the mountain looks to be a gentle slope, too."

We were very excited about our discovery. Over lunch we planned our adventure. If we could cut the trail before July 1, we could put our ranging cattle up onto the alpine before the noxious milk vetch would come into bloom.

Speed was required. We figured it would take two days. If we left early in the morning, we could accomplish a lot and be home for a late supper both nights. The babysitter, a sweet, dependable teenage girl the boys loved, would do the ranch chores with four-and-a-half-year-old Marty's help, while Barry went along in his buggy.

Grandpa sharpened up his double-bitted axe and swede saw. I packed a big lunch, two quarts of water and two coats for the evening onto our gentle pack horse and we were off.

In an hour we were at the burned-over ridge. The new growth of pines was only about three feet high among the bare, blackened windfalls. Grandpa had only to cut three dead, limbless pines lying across the ridge.

Then we met the grassy bench, which was only fifteen feet wide. A spring oozing out of a bog as we went north gave us a mucky crossing, but the bottom was gravel. Only two hundred yards ahead we topped out onto a bald, grassy knoll with a grand view of the whole valley.

We unsaddled all three horses, unbridled them and let them drag their six-foot halter ropes to roll and then graze their lunch while we had ours. It was a beautiful, late June day and there was a light breeze and puffy white clouds floating in a very blue sky.

We cleared a trail so we could let our cattle graze in the meadow on top of Potato Mountain.

Soon it was time to get back to work. Looking south, the escalating ridge was rock on the down side, but thick with fifteen-foot pines on a narrow strip of ground—it was made to order for a perfect trail, once we cut all the pines.

We resaddled our horses, and I led them while Grandpa cut the young trees. I helped by throwing them, spearlike, through the thick forest below the trail. It was steep and deep to the creek gurgling in a timbered valley below.

The cleared trail grew ever longer, and it was a thing of beauty just waiting to be uncovered by KB, the worthy pioneer. By 4:30 we called it quits and Grandpa tied his axe onto the pack horse so he could have his hands free for the reins.

It didn't take much time to ride the four miles home, as it was all downhill. The horses sipped water at the spring, taking turns to prevent muddying the water. We went down the burned ridge and through the timber and walked in to a hot supper cooked by our babysitter, who delighted in the account of our day.

After a good night's sleep, Grandpa and I saddled up to go finish the trail. This time we took our sleeping bags as we didn't know if we would get it finished that day. We told our babysitter not to worry in case we had to stay overnight.

The horses seemed to enjoy going up our new trail, and so did we. When we got to the place we had stopped working the day before, KB started removing the trees from the gentle grade while I loosened the cinches a bit on the horses to make them more comfortable. Then I began throwing the trees down into the creek canyon below.

By 1:00 p.m. we had reached the top and come out onto a small, level meadow. There was one last strip of alpine forest that was about fifty yards wide, but within an hour we were welcomed by open meadows.

We unsaddled to let the horses roll and graze. We enjoyed our lunch while looking out at the grassy hillsides bordering both sides of the flat meadowland. A small lake glinted at us about a half mile away.

We were justly proud of our efforts, and we knew our cowherd would do better up here in the true alpine.

After lunch we saddled up for a rideabout before leaving. To get an idea of the size of the north end, we rode up to the south side and looked over the west rim. Wowee! What a view. The fifteen-mile-long Tatlayoko Lake and much of the valley floor lay below us. Across the valley we could see more of the Niut Coast Range from our 6,500-foot elevation. How tiny the settlers' fields appeared in all this vastness.

Leaving our horses to graze, we took a short walk along the rim and what we found dumbfounded us. A bank, eight feet high and thirty yards long with a flat six-foot walkway out in front, was completely composed of seashells! The bank was solid white with no dirt among the shells. We pocketed a few samples. Sadly, neither of us had a camera.

We returned to our horses and back to our packsaddle, where we loaded up and rode our new, well-groomed trail off the mountain. We would be home for supper after all.

We hired a young fellow who was eager for adventure to round up the cattle and help put them up the new trail. Three days later we had most of them. Grandpa and I pushed eight head as leaders up the trail for the rest to follow, driven by our hired cowboy.

The next few days kept us busy rounding up the dozen we missed and introducing them to the trail. We packed up two fifty-pound blocks of salt to put out on gravelly knolls to prevent hoof damage to the alpine herbage, and we rode up once a week to check on predators.

Because it was such a delightful adventure, I began advertising for families to take trips up there. For several years we benefitted twofold: the cattle thrived, and I had fun sharing this beautiful alpine spot while being paid for it.

## OUR FIRST GUEST CABIN

Long before I got to the ranch, when KB was still married, his brother-in-law, Percy Church, decided to join KB and Dolly at Circle X.

Percy built a sizeable one-room log cabin just uphill from Tatlayoko Lake, which provided a spectacular view of its turquoise-blue water and the Coast Range. The cabin was backed by a forest of healthy old fir trees, and a little stream ran in a draw directly below it.

When I arrived in 1940, Percy was long gone. The cabin stood empty, but the ditch still ran water, which fascinated me, as it appeared to be running uphill! I knew that would be defying gravity, but the angle of the ditch against the angle of the sidehill gave that impression.

When I first moved to the ranch I wanted to know more about the cabin, so I asked KB, "Does Percy still come to holiday in his cabin?"

"No, he's not come for ten years or so," he replied. "He got married and he's involved in his own family life."

"So the cabin just sits there weathering away?"

"Yes, that's right," he said.

By now KB was using the cabin for guests during his seasonal guiding/hunting operation. In 1950 he phoned Percy with an offer to buy it from him and he agreed.

KB wanted to move the cabin closer to the ranch so we set

about numbering each log before taking it apart and hauling the logs home. This was done in the winter when sledding was easier on the horses. We would be situating it out beside the seldom-used road, with lots of parking space and a super view of the mountain range just across the valley.

In the spring, KB poured a concrete base and then re-assembled it to become his one-room guest cabin, with a full-width porch and a new roof. We furnished it with a heater and cookstove, four bunks, a table and chairs, a set of dishes and two kerosene lamps. It had everything a person could need, and our guests in the summertime or during hunting season all liked the privacy it provided. Guests often sat out on the porch with binoculars to watch the mountain goats.

This cabin marked the beginnings of my affinity for acquiring cabins. I would build or buy many of them over the next fifty years.

## RANGE RIDING: THE UPSIDE OF COWBOYING

Once a week it was my job and my pleasure to ride my saddle horse pal Joey down range twelve miles or more to check on our cow and calf herd.

One May morning I was awake before daylight, as usual, to build up the cookstove fire and then head out to the corral to give my Joe-horse his oats treat. The sky was lightening and the grass was dewy; it was going to be a lovely day.

Back inside, my cast-iron fry pan was ready and hotcake batter was soon sizzling on a smear of bacon grease. With a brace of eggs to follow, my body was fortified for the long day ahead.

My two little sons were still sleeping. Marty was six now, and Barry was four and a half. They would be safe in the care of their doting grandfather, whom they now called "Poppi." I could hear him stirring around now.

While I was plastering two surviving hotcakes together with strawberry jam—my lunch, to go into my pocket—Grandpa entered the kitchen. We sat down with our morning coffee to discuss the plans for the day. I never left without telling Grandpa where I was going. It was the rule. Today would be a long ride and I wouldn't be back until evening.

With a light jacket, chaps, my number ten beaver cowboy hat and gumboots, I collected my 30-30 rifle and seven shells and headed out to the corral.

Saddled and bridled, Joe and I left as the first rays of the sun lit the Niut Range west of Tatlayoko Lake. Our trail left all roads and civilization behind as we entered the poplar- and fir-studded slopes of our spring range. The warming air was redolent with the perfume of coniferous needles drying in the sun on the ground. If one could bottle that scent it would top the market!

Golden balsamroot blossoms gilded the greening hillsides, their large sunflower faces slowly wheeling to follow the sun. A few birds were still atwitter, though many had established their territorial rights and settled down to serious housekeeping.

Within a couple of miles we came upon our first cattle. It was a few young mothers, white-faced Hereford heifers with their first calves. The heifers hungrily cropped the new grass while their calves frisked about, playing tag and butting heads. One or two wise older matronly cows raised their heads to check us out, but they knew Joe and me and they went back to grazing at the sound of my voice.

Everything appeared normal, and there were no big teats that needed milking out. We only had to do that when there was an overabundance of milk that was too much for a newborn calf. If the cow isn't milked out by the herder, that teat spoils, and when the calf is older and needs four quarters, it has only three.

The older cows, who calved out first, had drifted further down range to search out their familiar clover-patched haunts. Joe needed no urging, as he knew all of the trails and was content and happy in his role, as was I.

We were riding the grassy hillsides between stands of timber when I saw an animal lying out on the grassy hillside. A dead animal? A bear kill? We approached a Hereford yearling steer lying flat out. I dismounted and dropped the reins so Joe could graze.

The yearling's eyes were open and milky white. He was still

breathing with no sign of rips to his hide and no broken legs. So what, then? Then I found it. I ran my hands over his body and his poll was crusty with tick bodies.

We had been dehorning before turnout and he had knocked the scabs off of both horn stubs, thrashing around in his efforts to rise. The flies had invaded and laid eggs, but they hadn't hatched yet. By now, the ticks had him paralyzed, and the sun had almost blinded him.

I took out my Stockman pocketknife and scraped the ticks from his head, squashing them between two stones. Next, I cleaned out the horn cups and wiped them out with grass. Fortunately, I had brought a small salt shaker for my hard-boiled eggs so I liberally salted them and packed them with moss.

This steer was woolly with his winter coat but I knew he wasn't ours. His ears didn't bear the Circle X Ranch sign on the tips. I realized that he was our neighbour's yearling. We had been asked to feed him over the winter.

By now the steer was moving his legs in an effort to rise. Good, I thought. He would make it yet. But he was going to need help. I tied Joe in the shade and loosened his cinch a bit. Then I rolled the yearling up into a semi-sitting position, and yet again when he flopped down. We repeated this until he regained the use of his muscles, and within fifteen minutes he was standing shakily. He didn't know me, so he kept struggling to escape, which our own gentler animals may not have done.

As soon as his trembling legs would hold him, he tried to get away from me, but he needed bracing up. I buried my fingers in his shaggy winter coat and together we traversed that hillside as an inverted V-shape as I leaned into his five-hundred-pound frame to keep him upright while he got his legs under control. A glint of water shone below us from a pool of spring runoff.

Good. He needed a drink. I decided we'd go down to it. I angled his course, and by then we were going at a slow trot. We reached the pool, but he kept walking through it and didn't stop for a drink. The water ran over into my gumboots. We staggered through it and out onto level ground under big, shady fir trees. He was much better, so I left him there and waded back through the pond to the hillside and returned to my horse.

We continued on down range for another mile to where the main herd was grazing on a bunchgrass hillside. They were quiet and content. There were no bawling cows calling hopelessly for calves that had been lost to bears. I would pack some salt blocks down to them within a day or two.

I had a gunny sack with me, so I filled it with sweet, green bunchgrass for the steer I'd left across the pond. Returning to the spot, there was no sign of my steer friend. I dumped out the grass for some lucky doe mother to find and rode back to the ranch.

Along the way, I mused about how lucky that steer was that eagles, bears, coyotes or wolves hadn't found him in his helpless condition. I later heard that our neighbour brought that steer to the cattle sale in the fall and got a good price for him.

What a story I had to tell to Grandpa and the little boys when I got home.

# RECORDING HISTORY

In September of 1953 the building of a new road to Bella Coola was in its second and final year. It was the talk of the Chilcotin, and people were tracking the progress. For months folks had been saying, "It's already finished!" while others said, "Maybe next week!"

I knew this was history being made, and I thought someone should be recording it. KB had bought me a windup movie camera for my thirty-first birthday and I was quite competent with it by now. So I figured, why not me?

It had been a busy summer and the tame hay was ready to cut at the home ranch. Since Grandpa hadn't been feeling well, he had hired a haying crew to put up the clover and timothy hay at the ranch. I was glad he would get a rest this fall as he had been ill for a while and had started throwing up his meals. We drove to the Williams Lake hospital where a doctor diagnosed stomach ulcers and put him on a milk-and-eggs diet and sent him home. He couldn't keep that down either, so we knew he needed a thorough examination.

I contacted our friend Tom, who owned Chilko Lake Lodge and flew a plane. He agreed to help, and he flew into our airstrip and took Grandpa to the Shaughnessy Hospital for veterans in Vancouver. They admitted him and let us know he was to stay in the hospital for at least a week under observation.

The boys and I were sure that he would come home cured. He was strong, and nothing ever daunted him.

The weather was fine and we needed a distraction from our worrying, so I started thinking seriously about making the trip to record the road building. My mind totalled up the days it might take and I figured it would probably be four or five.

I decided to take my boys with me, so I called them in to run it by them. "Oh boy, Mom!" they said. "That'll be fun!" They got our horses so we could ride to the meadow to check with the crew. I explained my plan to the crew and told them I would be back in four or five days. "What do you think? Will you all be okay?" I asked.

"Go for it!" they cheered.

The boys and I rode the six miles back home, turned our horses into the pasture, fed extra feed to the chickens and made lots of jelly and peanut butter sandwiches. We packed up food, extra clothes and sleeping bags, checking everything off my list as we loaded it into the pickup truck. We would leave early the next morning.

The next day we drove about eighty miles to Trail's End Lodge, south of Anahim Lake, where I rented two saddle horses. Our light sleeping bags were tied on and the food went into bags hanging from my saddle horn. Baptiste Elkins, a police officer for the Anahim Lake Reservation, was having a Sunday visit with the neighbouring lodge and we couldn't believe our good luck when he offered to guide us to the starting place of the new road, which had been made the previous year.

At sundown he guided us through the jack pine forests and around swamps. There was still some daylight when he led us to a grassy meadow where we were to spend the night. "Here's pasture for your horses," he said. "And last year's Cat track starts just fifty yards over there. You can't miss it. Just follow it to the timber, and the trail is clear from there."

We thanked him for guiding us, and he rode off to the reservation, which was a half mile away.

There was one lone spruce tree there on the meadow. We unsaddled our gentle horses and staked them out on the meadow. We unrolled our sleeping bags, snuggled them up under the spruce tree and ate sandwiches before crawling into them. There were a few raindrops spattering down by then. I stacked my loaded rifle against the tree before we fell asleep—this was bear country!

We were up at dawn, and we saddled our horses, tied on our sleeping bags and rode along the Cat track toward the forest ahead. The grass track led us to the bulldozed trail, a muddy, narrow track with trees laid over against the forest on both sides. It didn't look like much, but it was the start of the road-to-be that was built with courage and determination.

We fed and watered the horses and ourselves at Green River, rested an hour and arrived by sunset that day at the road workers'

After months of bulldozing and moving rock, the two Cats met.

camp. If the crew was surprised by our arrival, they didn't show it. Alf, the D6 Cat operator, invited us to have supper, then gave us a huge tarpaulin to soften the stony patch of level new road. I knew who he was, as he worked for the Grahams.

We laid out our three sleeping bags, then folded the rest of the tarp over our bags, crawled in and slept soundly.

For the next day and a half I kept busy shooting history in the making with my fixed-lens, 8-mm windup camera. Watching this cool-headed Cat operator blast that eighty-degree rock mountainside, then push and scrape the rubble to the very edge of a thousand-foot drop, was terrifying. I marvelled at his nerves of steel.

It was difficult to get it all in with my fixed lens. So I climbed up that almost vertical mountain slope and crawled out on horizontal tree trunks that were hanging by a root or two over the canyon

The historic moment. Alf Bracewell (left) shakes hands with the Bella Coola bulldozer operator, George Dalshaug.

while trying to hold my 8-mm camera steady to get the action.

There was lots of drilling, using fourteen holes with a compressor. They stuffed them with dynamite sticks, then blasted a ledge for the new road. The boys and I ran the two-thousand-foot horizontal goat-trail along the still virginal mountainside between camps to film the Bella Coola crew as they drilled and blasted their way to meet with Alf and his crew and complete the road.

Back at Alf's camp we all had supper together again, and then the boys and I retired to our sleeping bag beds on the historic road. Our wilderness guide, Officer Elkins, had appeared that day with a male teacher for Bella Coola. The teacher would be catching a ride down the mountain the next day in the Jeep the Bella Coola work crew used.

We would be leaving the next day too, so I left my movie camera with Alf to have someone record the meeting of the Cats from the opposite directions in two weeks. This was done, I would eventually discover, very capably, with my remaining twenty-five feet of film.

Riding back toward Anahim Lake with Officer Elkins, the boys each had a horse as the

The road opened up travel between Williams Lake and Bella Coola.

teacher's horse had to be returned. It was about thirty miles, and it didn't seem so far on our return trip. When we parted from Officer Elkins, the boys doubled again on the lodge horse. We gave both horses their heads and didn't rein them so they could go home to Trail's End Lodge and reunite us with our pickup.

We thanked the folks there and told them details of our adventure. It was a thrill to create a documentary of the actual live action of that road being built, so I was happy we were able to do it.

We reached home late that night and were very happy to sleep in our own beds. The next day we put things on the ranch back into working order. I separated the cow and calf for the day, got my horse in to go see the hay crew and got the kids back to school. We expected Grandpa to return from seeing the doctors at Shaughnessy any day now.

## THE DIAGNOSIS

Two days later Grandpa returned from the Vancouver hospital with devastating news. The Shaughnessy Hospital doctors had discovered that he was full of cancer and predicted that he would live only another two months. Grandpa explained it all to me very matter-of-factly and said he came home to put his affairs in order.

I was devastated and in complete shock, and I had to go off by myself to vent my disbelief, desolation and anger at the world. I saddled my horse and rode away quickly to get away from any possibility of being heard by others.

When I was out on the range, about two miles from the buildings, I rode blindly, screaming, weeping and beseeching God to overturn that fatal diagnosis. I begged that the doctors could be proven wrong. I pleaded that this kind and generous-hearted man had rightfully earned a longer lease on life, that now, in his golden years, he should be allowed to enjoy his grandchildren, since he was denied the pleasure of being with his own children while they grew up.

When I had exhausted myself I rode back home. Around my little boys and their Grandpa I tried to maintain my composure, following Grandpa's cheerful example. He refused to dwell on the impending doom, concentrating on the daily tasks at hand, and I would have to learn to do the same.

Grandpa remained undaunted. He maintained a positive spirit, getting about as usual, driving his grandsons to the school and going back to bring them home again. He made kites to fly during our notorious Tatlayoko winds. It was so heartwarming to watch. Freed up from ranch chores by his hay crew at the meadow and the daily chores at home, which I insisted on doing so I could keep too busy to think, Grandpa indulged himself by baking his famous cornbread johnnycake to serve with moose roast and beans. He kept the boys entertained with snatches of songs or rhyming ditties he had learned as a child.

He was surprised and excited to hear that the two boys and I had ridden by horseback the thirty miles to Alf Bracewell's camp to record the building of the Bella Coola road. He was just delighted that I had used the windup movie camera he had bought me for my birthday

"You put it to very good use by recording that historical event. I'm so proud that you did that!" he said. Grandpa was big on preserving history.

The work on the ranch needed to go on, and it was time to gather the beef to send to the October sales. While I went out riding every day I searched for answers to the reality of Grandpa leaving us soon. It was almost impossible to consider. What would happen to us then? Grandpa was always my mentor: he'd taught me so much over the past thirteen-plus years about living a pioneer's life. He was genuinely concerned for my welfare and that of his grandsons, and he knew we would be alone soon. He faced that fact, which forced me to face it too.

But how? I had no plan. Grandpa was my father figure, and after Bev left and crushed Grandpa's bright hopes of his son and the rest of us all being a family, we had continued our lives together and run the family ranch. This place was his pride and joy that he had wrestled from the wilderness by hand, with one team of horses and stumping powder. He had built up a handsome herd of near-purebred Hereford cattle and built a new log house, guaranteed to stand a hundred years. I knew his dearest wish was to see his life's work continue so his grandkids could enjoy the lifestyle he had built over the years. But I didn't know how it was all going to work out.

Grandpa wanted very much to visit his family members in New Mexico before he died. He had not seen them in forty years. I knew I needed to make that happen. We would figure out a way for him to go after the cattle sale on October 9.

One late September afternoon, when I returned to the ranch with a few stray cattle, Grandpa and the boys helped put my horse away. Fresh coffee and warm johnnycake was waiting for me and right away I wondered what was up.

When I was warm, fed and comfortable, Grandpa divulged his scheme. And when I heard it, I was, for once in my life, speechless.

Somehow Grandpa had gotten a message out to Alf Bracewell, who was now back at Graham's ranch with his D6 Cat, to come and see him when he was back from building the Bella Coola road. There was no phone, and mail was twice a month, so I'm not sure how he managed to contact him, but he did.

Alf had arrived the day before while the boys were in school and I was looking for cattle, so I was not privy to their conversation. Grandpa told me he had poured a cup of coffee for both Alf and himself, then told Alf he had a proposition for him. "Alf, I don't have much time left," he said. "I'm worried about Gerry. She can't run this ranch alone. Would you consider becoming her business partner? But before you answer, I must warn you, the ranch owes the bank eighty thousand dollars."

Alf chewed his tobacco and took a sip of coffee while he considered this.

"Well, I guess I could," he said finally.

"Well, Alf, I have some shares to sell. Do you have any collateral?"

There was another long pause, as Alf was never one to hurry into anything. "Well," he said. "I've got two quarter sections and some stock and equipment."

"Would you consider selling your collateral to buy my shares?"

"Well, I guess I could do that," Alf said.

131

They had drawn up a contract on the spot, which Grandpa would register on his next trip to Williams Lake.

I did not know much about Mr. Bracewell except that he worked for Bill Graham and, of course, that he had been operating Bill's Cat, bulldozing the road to Bella Coola. When I met him during my trip to document the road building, I was very impressed by his cool courage and calculations on that very dangerous job. And now he had agreed to buy Grandpa's shares in the ranch. Unbelievable!

Grandpa had chosen a man that he admired and trusted to sell his shares to, and I respected Grandpa's judgment and decisions.

Alf gave notice to Bill Graham, and they were extremely sorrowful for the events happening to KB. They felt that Alf was doing the right thing by stepping up to the plate and they wished him well.

Alf Bracewell had become the life preserver I needed to solve several immediate predicaments I was facing. I knew I needed to get Grandpa off to go see his family while he was still physically able. I wanted to drive him to town, buy him a ticket and see him on his way, and the sooner, the better. But the cattle sale was impending ...

# THE NEW BUSINESS PARTNER ARRIVES

Grandpa had told me to expect Alf Bracewell to come to see me sometime in October to take on his new job as my business partner. Without a telephone I didn't know exactly when to expect him. While I awaited his arrival, I reviewed what I knew about him. Alf was a well-built man, tall, with broad shoulders and a reputation of being a responsible, dependable fellow, with a chuckle and quick, quiet humour.

One day when Grandpa and the boys had left to walk down into the field to look at the beef cattle, Alf arrived. I welcomed him in and we sat down to coffee. I asked him if he was glad the Bella Coola road was finished.

"It needs a lot more work to make it into a highway," he said.

I said, "It was plenty high for me!" and he chuckled.

"Alf," I said, "I sure appreciate you agreeing to Grandpa's offer. I know it's more than I can handle. I respect Grandpa's decision. Also, I admire you for your courage in taking on this business partnership. I'll do all the cooking and the riding. My boys do the chores, like the chickens, wood and water, and they ride with me when they're not in school. I know you'll see lots of room for improvement: fences, for one thing. I'm not going to give orders, I respect your judgment, but I'll answer any questions you have, okay?"

"Fair enough," Alf said. "Where do I sleep?"

"There's a cool, big basement room for hot weather, and a

Alf was a welcome addition to the operation. He was an experienced rancher and adept at roping calves.

Below: Gerry throws a calf for branding. It was a team effort.

warm upstairs bedroom for cold weather, take your pick. The boys and I have our rooms off the kitchen on the main floor, and Grandpa has his bed beside the furnace."

"Well, I'll bring my duffel upstairs, since winter is coming on," Alf decided.

Grandpa and the boys came in then, and Grandpa and Alf shook hands. "Do you recognize this man, kids?" I asked.

"Sure! You're the guy that drove the Cat after you blew up the mountain!" eight-year-old Marty said.

"Well, boys," I said. "This man is going to help us run this ranch, isn't that right, Grandpa?"

KB nodded.

"So if Mr. Bracewell asks you a question about where something he needs is at, you'll tell him or show him, okay?"

They both nodded.

"Call me Alf," he said.

The next day was Sunday, so Alf and the boys did a walkabout to look at the fences and check out the machinery. The kids came

Milking a cow because her calf was too young to drink from all the teats. This was a range cow and she was a bit jumpy. It was important not to sit on a stool while milking, so I could jump out of the way if she acted up. I would also tie their legs so she couldn't kick me.

back rosy faced and chattering with Alf like he was their uncle, and that took a load off my mind.

Eventually Alf took over the job of getting the kids to school, as well as the neighbour's kids, just like Grandpa did. He brought them back too, which freed up time for me at home.

Knowing Grandpa would be leaving soon to visit his family, I put on an open house party for him in the ranch house. I cooked up lots of food and baked bread and cakes. The house was filled with good friends and neighbours coming to visit with him for the last time. He was more ill and weaker by then and reclined on a double bed, set up in the large front room beside the big windows so he could be a part of it all. He reigned as Master of the Mansion and was honoured by all throughout the evening.

## GRANDPA FLIES TO NEW MEXICO

Having solved his concerns regarding his grandsons, me and the ranch, I thought Grandpa might be ready to go see his family and I asked him if he wanted to leave right away or wait for the cattle sale. I personally felt he should leave right away while he could enjoy the trip and physically handle it alone. With the two-month diagnosis, time was of the essence. But Grandpa surprised me again.

"I don't care about the sale itself," he said. "It's the preparations here at the ranch that give me pleasure. You coming home with a herd, running them into the barnyard to separate the steers and old dry cows. The animals, the noise, the smells, the dust—that's the memory I want to take with me. And you hungry, hardworking cowpokes coming in for my johnnycake and fresh cow's milk! So if Alf wants to help you finish the roundup, let's get the sale over, then I'll go with you to the airport. Alf can stay and catch up with the boys. Besides, I'm enjoying my grandsons so very much, I'm not about to cut that short until I have to. Okay?"

"Okay," I agreed.

That evening I had a talk with Alf and told him what Grandpa had said about how much he was enjoying our corner of the "Old West" and how he loved the cattle being brought home, the cowboying, the dust and the bellowing of the cows. We would change the original plan to fit with Grandpa's wishes.

"You know what, Alf?" I said. "This is his last fall to experience the roundup; he could even take in the sale on the ninth with good rests in between. He thought both of us should ride to clear the range for the next couple of days. How about it?" We would be trucking our cows to the sale for the first time in Circle X history, and I knew Grandpa would want to see that.

"Okay by me," Alf agreed.

So I told Grandpa our plan. "Both Alf and I will ride for two days. Load the two trucks on the seventh at home here. We'll pack your suitcase and drive in on the eighth, get two hotel rooms at the Lakeview, and enjoy some of the sale between rests. How about that?"

"Sounds fine to me," Grandpa said.

We would be shipping two loads. Over the next week of working with Alf, I noticed how he made every move count, yet appeared to be relaxed and never agitated or confused. He never seemed to tire at whatever needed to be done, be it repairing a fence, rounding up cattle, cutting a supply of stove wood and splitting it or driving the boys to school.

We hired a local girl to help with the housework to free up Alf for his ranch repairs and I did the Circle X chores. Grandpa and I would go to the sale. It was better for the owners to be present, Tuffy Derrick, our field man, pointed out.

Grandpa and I left by pickup truck for Williams Lake. It would be 165 miles of mostly gravel road, so we had plenty of time to talk. I thanked him for his perspicacity in sizing up the situation and doing something about it.

He smiled at my word choice. Our favourite game on a nasty day was trying to stick each other by using and spelling unfamiliar words correctly. He said how happy he felt that I had accepted his solution to the problems of trying to hold it all together.

We got into town late, took rooms in the Lakeview Hotel, had a meal and retired for the night. We would go to the airport in the morning to book his flight to Albuquerque for the tenth.

The next morning we had a nice breakfast, then we rested before getting Grandpa's lawyer to register Alf's agreement. Grandpa was now on a special diet that agreed with him. We shopped for food items he was used to rather than chance the menu on the plane.

Finally, ticket and transfers in his pocket, he felt that he really was going to see his family—after forty years! He could not believe it.

"But first, Grandpa," I said, "we are going down to the stockyard."

Tuffy Derrick greeted us at the sale ring and told us our cattle would arrive soon. Within a half hour, a uniform group of classic Hereford steers crowded into the sale ring. They were ours! The auctioneer used the short written history of our steers I had written: "Here's a nice group of long-yearling steers [that meant 1.5 years] from the Circle X Ranch, Tatlayoko Lake. These steers have spent two summers grazing on the subalpine Meadows of Potato Mountain. They are gentle, can be worked on foot. We'll start at forty cents per pound. Do I hear forty-five?" A yell from the bid-spotters claimed the bid: "These healthy young animals are now going at forty-five; forty-five; forty-five—look at their fur coats! These gentle steers are ready for winter; forty-five?" Another yell went up: "Now we have fifty—do I hear fifty?" A buyer signalled he was bidding higher and Grandpa grinned.

"I now have forty-eight, forty-eight, forty-eight! I tell you, you can't go wrong on these gentle, healthy animals. Fifty cents? Fifty cents; fifty cents! Sold!"

Now Grandpa was chortling. He waved to the auctioneer, whom he knew, and received a salute in return. The steers were driven out the gate to a pen; the buyer's name was posted on it.

Grandpa was ready to leave; he had had a fine time and had met with a few old friends. The salute from the auctioneer made his day.

The next day we had lunch at our hotel, and when we were done Grandpa was ready for a nap, which I knew could last until about four o'clock. I went out to do a little walkabout. The railroad station was just across the road and downhill from the Lakeview Hotel. I loved trains, just like my mom had. My brother Bob and I had travelled a lot with our mother when we were under five, and we rode for free across Alberta.

"When will the train be coming through?" I asked the telegrapher.

"I'm expecting it a little after four," he answered.

Good. I had time to check out the nearby stores before Grandpa's nap would be over.

First was Roderick Mackenzie's store. We bought almost everything from Mr. Mackenzie. He understood the ranchers' pay schedule and could wait until after the sale of cattle. He carried his rancher clients until then, which helped keep the small ranches going. I told him I had been at the sale, so if he could have our account ready, I could pay it in full before I headed home.

From there I crossed the main street to call in at Moore's Store and say hello to their three daughters, who were named Molly, Polly and Dolly, but they weren't in. There were a few more stores fronting on Railway Avenue, and I looked around a bit more before heading back to the Lakeview to be there when Grandpa awoke.

When he got up I asked him if he would like to be at the station when the Pacific Great Eastern came in.

"Yes! Let's do that!" he said. He loved the trains too.

We took our time walking the gravel road and steep slope to the station. The PGE (locally and jokingly called Please Go Easy and Plenty Good Eats, as fresh meats and vegetables were freighted in) was blowing its horn and ringing its bell, rolling in, panting and letting off steam as it rolled to a stop. Not many people were getting off, but a few got on to go north.

We stayed until it was leaving to enjoy the chug-chug-chug as it got steam up, blew its long, mournful whistle and disappeared further on around a bend.

"My!" Grandpa said, "wasn't that marvellous?"

Our whole time together had been marvellous, and Grandpa had seemed to absorb it like a kid storing up happy memories.

When I took him to the airport I hugged him and told him to phone me when he was ready to come home. I would come down to fly back with him.

He waved from the steps up into the plane. I stood there until the little plane was airborne, tears running down my face. Would I ever see him alive again? Of course you will, I told myself. Pull yourself together, woman!

After shopping for groceries, toys, chicken feed and sacks of horse oats, I paid Mr. Mackenzie then left for home. And what a long, lonely road it was for those 165 miles ...

My thoughts flew on ahead to the ranch. I wondered how Alf and the boys were doing. Were the range cattle drifting home? We would have to collect the cattle soon to pasture them on Skinner Meadow. I concentrated on the immediate problem, which was to get home safely. I was exhausted when I got back to the ranch at midnight, and I fell into my bed.

I woke in the morning and lay there for a while. I was used to waking early, but the events of the last few days had me so wrung out I wished I could just stay in bed for a few more hours.

I realized that the house seemed quieter than usual. Where were the sounds of my two boys running around? Then I heard low murmuring and a "shhh," and I realized who was in charge out there. Alf was keeping my exuberant boys under control and making sure they didn't wake me up.

I dressed hurriedly to join them. "Surprise!" Alf welcomed me with a big breakfast and the boys asked me lots of questions about the beef drive. After satisfying their childish curiosity, I dug out the single-bladed jackknives I had bought them from my bags, which brought excited whoops. They knew lots about knives, having watched deer and coyotes being skinned. Alf gave them each a stick to practise on and showed them how to safely open and close their knives to prevent cut fingers.

With the boys occupied, Alf and I could discuss my trip to town and Grandpa's safe departure, as well as the immediate state of the ranch affairs. It was so good to be home.

## GRANDPA COMES HOME

After a while, we got a message from Grandpa. He had enjoyed his long-anticipated visit with his family in New Mexico and was now ready to come home.

He was too sick to travel alone, so I would fly to Vancouver from Williams Lake, changing there for a direct flight to Albuquerque, New Mexico. I would pick Grandpa up and bring him home. I discussed my plan with Alf.

But Alf had his own agenda. "How about I drive us and the boys to Vancouver?" he said. "It would be good for the boys to see a big city, and for us to take a break."

"But what about the cattle?" I said. "Who would feed them?"

"I've already arranged that with Joe; he knows what to do." I relaxed and left it up to Alf. It was a great feeling to have someone else assume the responsibilities.

Joe had his work cut out for him for a week, at least. I cooked a big roast, extra bread, cookies and a stew for him, as he had to do the ranch chores, ride six miles to Skinner Meadow, catch up and harness the team of horses, drive them with the slip out to the stack, put on a load of hay, then drive in a circle while he pitched it off. Then he would ride back to the ranch, stoke up the fire so nothing would freeze, check the chicken pen for grain and water, close them in against predators after collecting the eggs, eat supper, go to bed and start all over again in the morning. It was a good thing he was strong and dependable.

We packed a change of clothes for each of us, some sandwiches and some quarts of water. We would stop overnight about halfway to Vancouver. We had just left Yale the next morning when Alf dropped his bombshell: "Why don't we get married while we're down here?" he asked.

I wasn't sure of what I'd heard with all the noise of the truck, so I said, "Pardon me?"

"I said, what do you think about us getting married before you fly to New Mexico?"

Well, I was speechless! What a strange proposal. It almost felt more like a business deal. I realized he had planned it all and given it a lot of thought.

I needed a few minutes. "Let me think about it for a while, okay?" I said. There were a few miles of silence. The two boys were sitting between Alf and me and they said nothing as Alf kept on driving.

I had seen how much the boys liked Alf. They followed him around and did whatever he asked. They had already learned a lot from him. He spent hours helping them with their homework, or asking them to spell words that sounded the same, dictating "Go through the door" and "Charlie threw the ball to me" while we all ate sandwiches in the shade with our saddle horses grazing nearby down on the range.

This was a big plus when I considered his proposal. I had admired and respected him since watching him building the road toward Bella Coola, and then there was the fact that Grandpa respected him and trusted him with the ranch. Alf certainly was a thinker; he did nothing on the spur of the moment, he was kind and considerate and a hard worker and he really liked my two boys, who were nine and seven by then. At thirty-two, he was tall, slim, handsome, blue-eyed and cheerful. I should be so lucky! All of these plusses added together and decided the future for my boys and me.

"Yes," I said.

We drove to the home of some good friends of mine on the outskirts of Vancouver. They had been to the ranch on two hunting trips and had also met KB and admired him. I had phoned ahead from Yale to let them know when to expect us. Thirza and Slim had a cozy home. They were delighted to see us, and Thirza showed us to our rooms. There was one for Alf, and one for the boys and me.

During the sumptuous meal she had prepared, I told them that Alf and I were engaged to be married—tomorrow—as I would be flying down to bring Grandpa home while Alf and the boys returned to the ranch.

"Could we be married here at your home?" I asked. Thirza and Slim.

"Of course! We'd be delighted," they said.

After our meal, while Thirza and I were doing the dishes, she asked me if we had the marriage licence.

"Heck no!" I replied. "He proposed to me on the drive here."

"Well, you do know that there is a three-day wait after buying the licence before it's valid?"

"Oh..." That was going to complicate things. Especially for the plan to pick up Grandpa.

"I will find a minister who does at-home weddings," Thirza said. She asked if I had a dress. "Of course not. He proposed to me in the truck," I said.

"No problem. We're the same size; you can borrow one of mine," she offered. "But you'd better get the licence first thing tomorrow, and don't forget to buy a ring, okay?"

Later that evening, while the boys were watching TV and Slim and Alf were talking about the Bella Coola road, Thirza and I visited their big bedroom.

We talked about the upcoming marriage and she asked me how committed I thought Alf was.

"My impression of Alf is, he applies due consideration to everything he undertakes," I said. "That's what attracts me; he makes no hasty decisions."

But afterward I mulled over my good friend's question. Later I asked Alf how he felt about helping to raise my sons. "Are you 100 percent committed?" I asked.

"They're great kids," he answered.

I asked how he felt about the responsibility of restoring the ranch, and the changes in marketing now that we didn't walk the cattle to the beef drives. I felt I was giving him serious reasons to change his mind.

To my surprise, he had a ready answer. "We will truck the cattle ourselves, and about replacing the fences and things, that's no big deal. We have a forest of fencing material."

After this very necessary talk with Alf, inspired by Thirza, I felt more secure with our commitment and I knew we were both on the same page.

We bought the marriage licence in the morning and then we crowded those three days with all the delights offered by a big city. We went to Stanley Park and the seafront with its big ships, and we looked at the tall buildings. The boys were googly-eyed at all the unexpected sights. We took them bowling, gave them rides on a beautiful merry-go-round and took a bus ride around the city. It was a trip to remember.

Alf bought a plain gold ring and Thirza found a minister. It was a quiet wedding with only the minister, Alf and me, our two friends as witnesses, and the two little boys as the audience. Thirza had prepared a lavish dinner, with wine for toasting the blushing bride and groom. Our honeymoon was short-lived, as my plane would be leaving for Albuquerque the next morning.

That morning I had another surprise: Thirza was going to come with me! Alf would stay with the boys, so I was grateful for the company and the moral support.

When we arrived, Grandpa seemed weaker and thinner than when he left. He was proud to introduce both of us to his brother, Paul, sister-in-law, Billy, and their children. Grandpa was so pleased that Thirza had come too.

Alf and I were married in 1953.

We left the next day. On the way, I told Grandpa that Alf and I were now married. He nodded his acceptance. He told me I had done right to marry Alf, who was a "real man" in his words, and "a good man" to help raise his grandsons.

Grandpa was not well at all. He accepted a painkilling shot on the way to Vancouver and by the time we got there I knew he was in no shape to go home to the ranch. Instead, Thirza and I took him back to the Shaughnessy Hospital.

The nurses remembered him: he had been a favourite because of his positive attitude and dry humour when he stayed there before. I left word for the staff to call me if anything changed, and I flew back to Williams Lake, where my new husband met me. Despite the sad circumstances of the last few days, the Graham family hosted a wedding reception for us at their home. Alf took a lot of roasting from his buddies, co-workers on the Graham ranch, but it was all in fun and good spirits.

We had returned home to full-blown winter and the hardships that ranching endures at forty below zero. I wrote a daily record of our doings at the ranch for Grandpa, who was to stay in the hospital, and sent it off to him at every opportunity, and the boys sent handmade cards every mail day.

## GRANDPA'S ISLAND

A few months later, in March, I got the dreaded telegram I had been expecting that said Grandpa was very sick and I needed to come. Early the next morning Alf gassed the truck while I made breakfast and packed my suitcase. I explained to the boys that their grandpa was very sick and needed me, but I'd be back soon. "Be good boys and help Alf, won't you?" I kissed everyone so long and drove off to Williams Lake to fly down to Vancouver with a heavy heart.

When I arrived, a nurse greeted me to take me to Grandpa's room. "How is he?" I asked. I was afraid to know.

"He's hanging on, waiting for you," she said.

It was a shock to see how emaciated he had become. I took Grandpa's frail hand in my rough one, squeezed gently and said, "I'm here, Grandpa."

He opened his blue eyes and smiled at me. From that moment on, a spark of life rekindled in him and glowed brighter every day that I was there, the nurses said. They thought it was a miracle. They all loved Grandpa because he was so gentlemanly, and so stoic with regard to his condition.

We had nine wonderful days talking and catching up on things. Several friends who had been his neighbours in Tatlayoko Valley but were now retired and living on the coast came to see him. I slept at the hospice beside the hospital, which was set up for out-of-town relatives.

During our conversations, he came up with a marvellous idea. "Gerry, one of my friends tells me there's an island just off the coast where someone left some cattle years ago. It might be for sale, and the cattle have multiplied so much they are overrunning the island. We could hire a few Chilcotin cowboys to run them onto a barge. We would have to build a wing fence like the Natives do, to trap wild horses to funnel them on. We could sell them to pay for the island. How about that?"

"Wow, Grandpa!" I said. "What a grand plan."

He suggested I go to the Lands Branch the next day to see what the story was with the island and whether it was for sale, and I agreed.

Unfortunately, I found out that the island had been settled up long before and that the cattle belonged to the landowners. The story Grandpa was told must have been from a long time ago. I had expected as much, but I didn't want to tell Grandpa.

"Well?" he asked me the next morning.

"I went to the land office," I said. "They checked out the island you mentioned. They are looking into the situation: who owns it, whether it is for sale. I'll go see them again in a day or two."

He was satisfied with that. I marvelled at this man, who left the easy, moneyed life of Boston to come to Canada at seventeen and live and pioneer. Even now he was still having his visions of adventure.

On the ninth day Grandpa was losing ground. I sat by his bedside late into the night. He and I had talked a lot about the hereafter. "Gerry," he had said, "When the time comes, I will try to tell you what I see."

I didn't want him to be alone when that time came, so from

that point on, I spent all of my days sitting in a chair beside his bed. That night I fell asleep, my head resting on his bed. A night nurse woke me up and led me to a small day room with a single cot where I could sleep the rest of the night.

At 6:00 a.m. I was up and back in Grandpa's room. He was hanging on, but his eyes didn't focus; they roamed independently about the room. I sponged his face and hands. He began making a rough sound as though he needed to clear his throat. A nurse came in, and I asked her to help me sit Grandpa up so he could clear his throat. She didn't offer to help, and instead left the room. Then a man came in and I asked him the same thing.

"Can I drive you somewhere?" he asked me.

I was confused. "No, thank you, I'm not going anywhere. Could we help Grandpa clear his throat, please?"

He left the room too, leaving me alone to deal with it.

The gargling noise continued, and then suddenly Grandpa reared upright, which he hadn't had the strength to do before. His blue eyes were wide opened and focused straight ahead at the blank wall across the room from him.

"Ohh!" he said loudly, and with such a note of incredulous wonder that I, too, looked at the wall.

"What is it, Grandpa?" I said. "What do you see?"

Still sitting upright, he said it again, "Oooh!!" And then he collapsed onto the pillow and he was gone.

He did his best to tell me, as he had promised. Had he really seen something? The nurse came in shortly after, and when she saw that he was gone, she asked me to leave. I wanted to take Grandpa's letters and belongings in his drawer, but she wouldn't let me.

I was now truly alone. My anchor was gone.

I don't remember much else about that day. I phoned his friends, and they knew what to do. Grandpa wanted to be cremated so his ashes could be scattered beside a lake in the wilderness he loved. We gathered at the crematorium for the service, and then I took his ashes home with me.

That summer his ashes were placed beside a small lake on top of Marmot Mountain.

## GOING HOME

Those three days after Grandpa passed away I was like a zombie, going through the necessary duties. After the service I caught a Greyhound bus to Williams Lake, where Alf met me. He had hired a neighbour lady to care for the boys and get them off to school each day.

After the events of the past thirteen days, I felt I had been rescued by my own guardian angel. When I saw Alf waiting at the bus depot, I almost lost it, but he grabbed my suitcase and hustled me to the truck away from the other passengers.

He began telling me about how things were back home. The boys were fine, there were five new calves, Joe was a great help. He said it all in a calm manner, which allowed me to keep control of myself. We bought a few things for the boys and headed for home. Spring had arrived, which was a distraction as the Chilcotin had been snowbound before.

The boys were glad to see us drive in. I hugged them to me tightly, then felt the grief coming on. Alf started preparing supper and I went for a walk down into the field to the cowherd, where I could finally let go of the pent-up misery stored up for too long. I wailed and sobbed to the cows. They regarded me wide-eyed and nervous, but they didn't move away from me.

The river was running free of ice, and I cupped the very cold water to wash my face. I let myself remember those last few minutes with Grandpa: how he had reared up to try and convey his vision to me. He had seemed thrilled at what he had seen—as though a door had opened on a new experience, a wonderful new adventure that he was being invited to join.

How could I not be happy for him? He had earned it.

Now my job was to carry on with the plan and raise the boys so they would enjoy what he had built. I needed to remember the good times we all had shared together and appreciate the steadying influence of Alf, which I was so thankful for.

It was time to return to the house. The kids and Alf would be concerned, but now I was purged of my misery and ready to carry on.

## THE NO-HAY WINTER

We missed Grandpa, but I tried to keep going and work hard every day. No matter how weary I was at the end of the day, or how peacefully my bed beckoned my spent body, my vigilant mind would be busy working on the plan for tomorrow or next week. Grandpa had always said, "Think ahead. Don't let circumstances trip you up."

I learned to think on my feet and reason things out, and when the hay didn't grow that summer, the plan came to our rescue, so we came through that winter with a handful of aces.

One day in August, Alf rode up to the big Skinner Meadow to check on the hay. But when he returned, he had bad news. "Well," he said, "the hay isn't high enough to cut. We will have to sell the cattle."

I could see the desperation in his face and my fighting spirit surged to the rescue. "Alf," I said, "there are more ways than one of skinning a cat."

We sat down with a pen and paper.

"First, the hay will require a machine to clear the snow away," I said. "Our horses do it every day when they are rustling and survive very well. I have heard of stray cattle following behind wild horses and surviving."

I started my list with "Number 1: bulldozer."

"If we feed the cattle grain everyday," I continued, "that will supplement their rustling and give them instant body heat and energy." That went down as number two.

"But do you realize how much a bulldozer costs?" Alf said. "How can we afford one?"

Ah ha, I thought. That's number three.

"We will pare down our herd and keep no replacement heifers. Let's hire a vet to preg-test our cows and sell all the empty ones. Every non-producer goes. We can sell the bulls, too, and buy them back in the spring. Then we can afford a bulldozer. And you have lumber from your sawmill to build troughs for the grain. You can snowplough the road to drive in the grain rations and clear enough meadow grass each day to feed the cattle. I have heard of this being done successfully."

I jotted down each money-producing prospect. It was a case of sacrificing some to save the core. But our pregnant herd of handsome Hereford cows, a near purebred strain built up over the years—sell them? No way!

We arose from the table with renewed hopes and the determination to carry it off.

Since we were freed up from haying Skinner Meadow, we decided to put those four weeks to good use by picking and preparing berries, harvesting the garden and getting in the winter wood supply. By now we had a pickup, so we cut the wood right out in the forest and hauled it home. On nice days we made a picnic of it, and on rainy days we stayed in and helped the boys with their lessons.

## HUNTING MOUNTAIN GOATS

In early September, Alf and I were hired to take two hunters on a mountain-goat hunt. Our neighbour's daughter would stay with the boys and look after the ranch house while we were gone for a week so Alf and I could go together. The two hunters arrived the day before the hunt and had supper with us, then retired to their cabin. The next morning we set out for the two-day trip, twenty-five to thirty miles to mountain-goat country. There was no road, only cow trails.

The weather was clear with no wind, perfect for a ride into the big mountains. In a way, I thought of the trip as being the honeymoon Alf and I hadn't had time for. But unlike most honeymoons that cost money, we were actually making it!

We camped the first night on a nice little meadow about fifteen miles from the ranch to be sure the horses were well fed for the arduous timbered trip the next day. I made the campfire on a level bare spot above the meadow, and Alf and the hunters set up the tents. I had prepared our supper at home, so we just heated up the tasty chili and had tossed salad and home-baked buns.

We sat around the fire for a while and shared some stories, and then Alf put a heavy log on to keep it going until morning and we all went off to our tents to be ready for the tough day tomorrow.

We got up early, ate and then packed up. This country was new to me and there was no trail, but the timber was old-growth fir and pine and where it grew thickest there was no bush to fight. We had two pack horses and our four saddle horses following each other through the dark forest, hoping we would come upon a meadow so our horses could eat.

As it became darker, Alf took out his flashlight to help him pick the widest spaces through the timber and the rest of us just followed, dodging limbs.

Then Alf stopped—or rather, his horse stopped and refused to go any further. He was a wise horse, even in the dark. "This is it," Alf called. We dismounted, unsaddled and tied our horses to trees.

There was no horse feed, nor any water. I got a fire going and took a large Rogers syrup pail to put on the coals so I could heat up the precooked stew meat while I added canned vegetables.

One of the hunters was opening the cans for me, then chucking the empty cans about fifteen feet away. When we didn't hear them hit the ground, we took the flashlight to go have a look.

Whooee! We were on the edge of a huge, thirty-foot-deep washout!

The fellows pulled their sleeping bags back down the trail, away from the edge, while Alf joked, "If either of you are sleepwalkers I'd better tie you to the trees."

Next morning we saw the immensity of this washout: thirty yards deep, thirty yards wide and three hundred yards long. We appreciated Alf's horse, whose sense had saved us from a serious accident in the dark.

The next morning, we found the meadow we had been looking for only a half mile beyond our camp. We unsaddled all the horses so they could roll and graze, and we made coffee with the clear, cool water of a nearby creek. Breakfast was delightful. After three hours we saddled up, packed the horses and rode on about seven miles to where the valley widened to provide a large meadow for the horses, a grassy bank with big sheltering fir trees, a little stream chuckling along downhill beside our campsite and

The terrain for goat hunting is quite rugged and challenging at the best of times. We couldn't hunt them after September because the snow and ice make it quite dangerous.

a mind-boggling view of the rugged, rocky mountain range, four thousand feet higher, just across the valley. We were now at an altitude of six thousand feet.

We all sat on the bank glassing the scene while the fire burned down to coals and the coffee brewed.

We had a quiet, peaceful day. The horses were knee-deep in lush meadow grass, and by 4:00 p.m. the sun was still shining over the timbered west rim behind us, lighting the massive mountain range out front. Just then a herd of mountain goats strung out single file among the ridges and cornices of that range. From that day on, this became our permanent campsite for mountain goats.

Hunting mountain goats is entirely different from hunting moose or deer, where you usually can't see them before they see or scent you. With mountain goats, you locate a loner, usually a billy, and memorize the vertical terrain he is feeding on, often one or two miles away up the rocks. By 10:00 a.m. he goes to his bed and stays put until 4:00 p.m. You have to plan your stalk with binoculars and check the clouds for wind direction up there. Once he goes to bed you have roughly six hours to get there and back.

We decided to wait until the next day, as it was already too late to stalk a moving goat. Meanwhile, we collected wood and I prepared food in advance for what would be our late return the next day.

Next morning we glassed the mountainside for a lone billy and got our horses ready to ride up as far as we could. I made lunches for each of us to tie in a coat behind the cantles of our saddles.

We located a billy bedded out on a pinnacle where he commanded a view of everything below him. It would be a tough stalk. We rode up through the timber to where it became steeper, unsaddled our horses and tied them to trees on level spots. I put a small bell on one to help us find them when the timber became darker in the evening.

We had chosen a ridge to hide behind as we climbed up, as we had to get above the billy. They were usually looking down.

The fellows drew grass to decide who would try for that goat. As he was bedded on a narrow rock spur, it was a long shot: 250 yards from the nearest cover. Alf and the hunter who won the draw started up, and the other stayed behind with me.

My hunter had a movie camera to film what was happening. From up there we could glass the whole range across the valley. Several hanging meadows trickled down between the ridges with little bands of nannies and kids visible.

Just when we thought the others may have decided it was impossible, we heard a rifle shot. We put up our binoculars to locate Alf and the hunter, and there they were climbing up the steep side of the pinnacle. It must have been a clean shot that killed the goat instantly. Anything less and the goat could have fallen to the rocks below and broken his horns off.

They waved us over and we walked out along the top of the ridge to join them. The billy was well furred and about eight years old, judging by the growth rings on his horns.

We congratulated the hunter and Alf for having made a very difficult stalk and such a good shot. Then we began skinning the billy. We took both hindquarters and the tenderloins to eat.

The descent of the mountain, loaded down as we were, was

Goats perch on steep pinnacles and rock faces, so it takes a lot of patience and good aim to hunt them successfully.

done slowly and carefully. Once we reached our horses, we could put the meat into plastic bags to tie onto our saddles. The hide was carefully rolled to enclose those sharp horns before tying behind Alf's saddle.

We got into camp just as the sun went behind our west range. There was still lots of skylight for camp chores and cooking supper. We would have tenderloin steaks in a day or two, after we let them tenderize a bit.

The next day Alf suggested riding up valley to learn more about it. I opted to stay at camp to protect our fresh meat, change the staked horses and do some cooking. I took a rest on the grass out front now and then, to glass for goats and to absorb the beauty of everything in sight: the green meadow, contented horses, the very green belt of timber clothing the flanks of that magnificent rocky range. The band of mountain goats was further along the mountainside toward the north now.

Alf and the hunters were back by five o'clock. I helped with the unsaddling and found the pelt of a second billy goat rolled up and tied behind the saddle of Alf's horse! He was a match for the first one. Hot coffee and cookies awaited the men and I heard about their day: they had seen herds of deer, with fourteen bucks bedded on a grassy slope to the left. As the men moved along beside the creek, the bucks stood up, stretched and moved uphill.

They saw a lone billy on the range to the right and—since the breeze was coming downhill toward them—it was an easy stalk up a bushy valley, then very cautiously up into the rocks to come out above the goat.

We had two very contented hunters in camp that evening. A big meal of pot roast, mashed potatoes, veggies and canned peaches disappeared quickly. Tomorrow we would pack up to return, but tonight we sat around the campfire until late, with only the crackling of the burning wood, the hissing of the gas lantern and the hoot of a lonely owl as background to the congenial conversation.

We all packed out next day and headed downhill, so we were home in time for a late supper. We boxed up their salted hides that night and they left happy the next morning.

# MILESTONES

When the boys started school, we had time to scour the range for any stray cattle. Everything except the beef cattle had to go to the meadow to graze the hay that was too short to cut. Then Alf trucked our beef to Williams Lake for the sale and hauled the grain home.

Alf bought an International TD-18 bulldozer to plough the deep snow we expected at the meadow. When winter came, we were happily surprised that the snow never got over twelve inches all winter. The cattle stayed warm pushing the loose snow with their heads to feed on the eight-inch hay underneath. We didn't have to build troughs for their grain, either. The cattle had packed the snow near to where they drank the creek's floodwater, so Alf just poured patches of grain on the packed snow. They became so smart! When they heard the truck motor, they all came for the grain, and as soon as it was gone, they went right back to rustling.

Now the cattle didn't have to wait at the empty stockyard, shivering in the cold wind, waiting for us to come and load up a slip and then feed it off to them. They kept warm and full all winter, and by March 10, when we brought them home to calve, they were in fine shape and well furred.

It had been a hectic year adjusting to life without Grandpa, but everything was working out okay. The boys were proud to have Alf as their stepfather, which made me very happy. He certainly was a naturally born father.

"Alf," I said to him one day, "you are such a good man with my boys, you should have some of your own, don't you think?"

He agreed and we consulted the calendar and decided that May was an ideal month for a new baby to arrive.

Things went according to plan. When our baby boy arrived on May 19 the next year, I was safely in the Williams Lake Hospital ... and Alf was stuck in a mudhole with a truckload of Circle X lumber eighty miles west at Anahim Lake, in his big three-ton cab-over truck.

We were thrilled, and we named our son Kevan Alfred Bracewell. By six months he could crawl up the stairway in the ranch house.

Barry holding his new brother Kevan.

## FENCING SKINNER MEADOW

In the fall of 1957 we were finishing up the haying of the Skinner Meadow. It had been a good crop, and there would be no shortage of hay for the cattle and horses this winter. We were lucky that Grandpa had been able to buy this thousand-acre meadow so long ago, as it had made it possible to build up a good herd of cattle with a large hay base.

The horses liked the meadow too. They preferred rustling their winter food to being fed hay, and the exercise kept them warm. Strangely enough, they had never left the meadow, even though it wasn't fenced, because the surrounding jack pines were so thick. KB had never had the time or the money to do it, and he wasn't worried about it because everyone knew the meadow belonged to him anyway.

But one October day a good friend of Alf's and mine who was from the Nemiah Reservation came and told us we needed to fence it. "Why?" Alf said. "Our animals never leave the meadow."

Our friend told us that he had been approached by a shady character who offered to pay him if he would drive our horses off the meadow in December so they would be illegally on the Crown range. He had a roundup permit from the government and he could legally take them.

We thanked him for telling us, but Alf told him not to worry. "If I catch anyone driving our horses off the meadow, I'll shoot his horse out from under him." And he meant it.

Nothing came of it, so we figured that message had been passed on to the would-be horse thief. But we still planned to fence the meadow in the late fall.

Alf bought a red roan Belgian gelding from the Graham family. He worked in harness and could pack a little. He was blocky, well muscled and very strong. We promptly named him "Uncle Bulgy." Alf hired a couple of men, and along with Uncle Bulgy, they became our fencing crew. The faller would hook him up to a log he had felled and start him on the skid trail in about seven inches of snow. Uncle Bulgy would deliver the log to the fence builders, about five hundred yards away.

They would lead him to where the fence needed that log, unhook the log, give him a scratch behind his ears and a pat on the rump and send him back along the trail to the faller. Uncle Bulgy never deviated from the skid trail to go off and munch meadow grass. It was uncanny to watch him plodding along with a log or returning to get another. He sure earned his extra ration of grain every evening.

We got the fence built in record time with Uncle Bulgy's help. It was five logs high with no barbed wire. Soon the wildlife, especially the moose, found sanctuary inside our fenced meadowland. It became useful as the roads improved and more and more resident hunters found their way into our wilderness. Without a fence, they might not realize the property was private land. Hunters were more respectful of a closed gate.

## A MAJOR RANGE IMPROVEMENT FOR THE CIRCLE X RANCH

My next brilliant brainstorm was to move our cattle from the north end of Potato Mountain to the south end.

Our neighbour, Joe Schuk, had ranged his cattle on Niut Mountain on the west side of Tatlayoko Valley. Several years before, when he had told Grandpa that a grizzly (or grizzlies) had killed six head of his cattle in the past week on that west Niut Mountain range, Grandpa, sympathetic as always, had invited Joe to bring his cattle over to the north end of our Potato Mountain range.

Well, it developed that there just wasn't enough feed for both herds. Also, it was a real chore to drift our herd to the extreme south end of their May/June spring range only to bring them fifteen to twenty miles back to put them onto that north end of Potato Mountain by July 15. We had to move our cattle away from the prolific milk vetch that was so poisonous to lactating cows, ewes and mares when in bloom.

We were very happy when the agrologist from Kamloops approved our request to increase our grazing to the south end of Potato Mountain.

I appealed to the Kamloops-based agrologist responsible for our area, explaining the vetch problem, the overstocked north end of Potato Mountain and the vastness of grazing on the south end that was utilized by only a small herd.

He and his brother drove up to do a range survey. I packed a horse with camping essentials for three days and saddled three more, and we rode off. They noted the vetch, now coming into bloom among the pine grass throughout the fifteen miles of our spring range. Then we took the cattle trail leading up onto Potato Mountain's south end.

Before two hours had passed we were riding through subalpine timber to break out onto lush mountain meadows, streams and two lakes, where I pitched our camp. It was one of my favourite places for hunting campouts, as it had all four necessities: horse feed and an area good for staking and hobbling our horses, a patch of balsam for shelter in case a gale-force wind blew in, dry wood for fires and, finally, water from a stream.

But the best part was the view. Looking across the mountain valley to the west rim, we were above seven thousand feet and above the timber line, so we could glass deer coming out to browse.

That day, not a cow was in sight.

Next day we rode over to McGhee's salt troughs. They were on a south slope beside a creek and were made of hollowed-out logs. The cattle grazed within a mile of this gathering spot all summer.

We made a wide circle, riding up into alpine meadows filled with lupine and Indian paintbrush. From there we could see the immensity of this alpine plateau. After checking the quality of the grazing throughout, we retired to our campout again to enjoy a meal of coal-baked potatoes, pre-roasted chicken, tossed salad and hobo fruit cake, which was baked at home in tin cans. It was the easiest cake to pack by horseback.

We had finished our range check and the weather had been perfect, not to mention the exhilarating scenery.

When we returned, a meeting of the ranching community was called. We all assembled in the evening the next day in Tatlayoko's little log schoolhouse. After a lengthy discourse on the fragile

Alf used his loader to plough a new cattle trail, but in the winter he also used it to clear the snow off the hay at Skinner Meadow so the cattle could graze.

quality of alpine meadows and the need to leave only one salt block per summer at each salting area, preferably on gravel with at least two miles between blocks, the agrologist delivered his decision: the south end could easily accommodate eight hundred head of cattle.

This was good news for us: between our neighbour's herd and ours, the numbers would not exceed three hundred head. We were most grateful to the grazing department for the go-ahead, and we totally agreed with the alpine-range management policies.

With our permit now signed by the agrologist, we herded our cattle up the mountain.

## THE FAMILY GROWS

Alf and I wanted to provide a playmate for our young son Kevan, who would soon be three years old, so we planned a second miracle. Alf was present when his second son, Alex Gordon, was born May 4, 1959, at Williams Lake Hospital. Alex was always smiling

161

Alex loved tinkering around the ranch, even at a young age.

I trained Alex (in the saddle) and Kevan at a young age to ride with me on the horse, so I could go check the cattle with my boys.

and cheerful, and his hair was so blond that he appeared to be bald. The older boys, who were fifteen and thirteen by now, enjoyed playing with their younger brothers, so our house was a happy, lively place.

I took time out to nurse Alex, as I had with Kevan, but by the time Alex was eight months old, I would take the little ones out with me on my faithful horse Sox to check the livestock like I did when my older boys were young. By then the big boys had become efficient cowboys, and Marty even rode a bronco in a rodeo. Alf was a great dad to all four boys. He was so patient with his teaching that they loved him. By the time Kevan and Alex were three and a half and six and a half, they were old enough to ride gentle horses alone with Alf and myself. Soon they would be following their older brothers' footsteps.

My guiding business was doing well, and I had started to invite other women and families along to enjoy the alpine with me. I was convinced to advertise this adventure, which became the "Soft Adventure" (no hunting) branch of my guiding business. This meant that more horses were required, so I bought young stallions and raised our own replacement stock. When they were four we gelded them ourselves and trained them to pack or ride.

I took school groups on June field trips as well, which I could do while watching over the cattle. Grizzlies preyed on our cattle on the alpine summer range, so my September 1 grizzly hunters eliminated any bear breakfasting on a cow he had killed. Wolves were prevalent also, but with me being there so often, accompanied by several talking and laughing riders, they moved on.

Sometimes early snow brought the cattle off the mountain before the permitted date of September 15. But there were always a few left that had to be sought out and driven down to their fall range to join the main herd in their homeward drift. My collie dog and I could manage the herd. A wave of the arm directed the dog to bring up the laggards, and no barking or yelling was necessary. Our presence was enough to maintain a cohesive herd. Having been heeled (nipped on the rear heels), the cattle developed a great respect for the dogs; their mere presence was enough to keep moving them along. There was a saying that "A good dog does the work of six cowboys—and peacefully." And it was true.

## MY TWO ELDEST SONS COME GUIDING

My two "sets" of sons fitted our lifestyle as if we'd planned it from the start. Alf was mentor and dad to all four boys. We had so much fun together, and all our holidays and birthdays were celebrated in Grandpa's big ranch house.

The boys were all given a good education outside of school as well: Alf taught them all about running heavy equipment and I taught them riding and guiding, packing horses, shooting. We never missed a local turkey shoot. I also taught them the art of socializing. With all our hunters and summer guests, the boys were exposed to a variety of interesting people from near and far, so good manners were high on my list.

By 1962 I was taking my two older boys on hunts with me. One time we were on a moose hunt on the north side of what would eventually become Bracewell Mountain, below Glacier Camp. We had two German hunters with us.

We made camp and my boys stayed behind while I took the two men out. One fellow was dressed to hunt, but the other wore a white shirt and a metal watchband that sparkled in the early morning light. The animals would see us coming a mile away, so I took off my muted green and yellow jacket to hang from a tree limb for cover so he could hide behind it.

I called the moose a couple of times and heard an answer that seemed to come from the Marmot Mountain Range, across the half mile of valley.

While I explained where to shoot a moose that was coming toward us, one of the fellows whispered, "Psst! Here he is!"

I looked across to my right and there was a bull standing right there. He had come up our trail on our scent without making a sound! He was probably the one who grunted.

Marty loved guiding and became a great companion and assistant on my hunting trips. This bear had been killing our cattle for fifteen years. Every time we encountered him at a fresh kill he ran away. We finally tied a cow to a post to draw him. When he was in range I had a clear shot.

I said, "Shoot him," to the man on my right. The moose was standing six yards from us. The man shot him. The moose kept standing there. I looked at the other hunter and said, "Your turn." He shot too and still the moose stood there. I looked at hunter number one and said, "Shoot again." To my amazement, the moose turned and staggered away!

He headed downhill through the young poplars and out of our sight, but I could follow his course by the shaking aspens as he wove his way downhill. None of us could believe it. "We will give him a few minutes before we follow," I said. "Those were point-blank shots. It's a miracle that he didn't charge us." We would have had a hard time escaping through the fire-killed, downed-timber groundcover and young second-growth pine.

In a few more minutes we started straight downhill on his trail. About three hundred yards down we came to an old logjam created by a snow slide fifteen to twenty years before.

There was the bull, all four legs jammed into the logs. He was dead, but still upright.

The men proceeded to break off two branch tips of a young pine, wipe the six-inch branches in the moose blood and stick them into their hatbands.

I was waiting until this ceremony was over, wondering how I was going to roll the moose onto his back out of that logjam, when my two sons showed up. Our overnight camp was only a half mile below the sound of the shots, so they had hustled right up to help. I surely was glad they had come along with me.

With all this help, we soon had the moose cleaned and ready. My two sons went back to the camp for the pack horses, while the hunters and I quartered the moose.

We loaded the pack horses to get the moose quarters into the cool, dark shade of the spruce forest nearby. We rigged a stout hanging pole from a strong, dry tree, horizontal and high enough that bears couldn't reach the meat, and hung all of it to cool out overnight.

While I cooked breakfast on the campfire, the hunters recited their heart-thumping experience to my boys, telling them all about how the bull had crept silently up to us and how he wouldn't go down at point-blank range.

They had taken pictures of him standing upright in the logjam, and of the bleeding and butchering.

After breakfast we laid about catching up on our rest. The hunters decided that one moose as big as a horse was all their little car could carry. Also, he was a joint effort, meaning each of them had shot him, yet he walked away, so neither could actually claim him. I could hear their story gaining momentum. It was sure to be a whopper by the time they flew home.

Since they were done with hunting, we told them about some good fishing lakes they might like to try. We could put their moose quarters, preboned and butchered, in our deep-freeze for when they were ready to take it home. They liked that idea.

Early the next morning, we packed camp and got their trophy moose home. We skinned and butchered the meat, then wrapped it for storing and freezing. Then we all went fishing for a little re-laxation after all that excitement.

## How I Met Leonard Billy

One morning in early June, I was returning home from Williams Lake where I had attended a meeting of the CTA (Cariboo Tourist Association) the night before. As I rolled up the hill approaching Alexis Creek in my pickup truck, there was the unmistakable sound of a flat tire.

I stopped the truck opposite the C1 ranch house to take a look and sure enough, the left rear was flat. I looked in the truck for the spare, but I couldn't find one.

Here I was, alone by the side of the road and dressed in my favourite magenta pantsuit with a white silk blouse. Oh my. It was 7:00 a.m. and everything was silent. Just then, while I pondered what to do, two Native men approached.

"You broke down?" asked the stocky one, who looked to be about in his late forties.

"Yes," I answered. "I've got a flat and no spare."

He looked in the box, then bent down and looked under the back end. Without another word he proceeded to extract the spare tire from its hiding place, found the bumper jack and the star wrench under the boxes of groceries and sacks of chicken feed and got right to work on the tire.

It seemed my guardian angel had been looking out for me. The man was quiet as he changed the tire and didn't speak again until he was tightening the wheel nuts. Then he said, "You got a ranch?"

"Yes."

"You need help?"

"Yes," I said. I told him my name, and he told me he was Leonard Billy of Alexis Creek Reservation.

I gave him breakfast money, along with my heartfelt thanks for his efficient help. I gave him a suggestion of how he could get to our ranch, telling him that Lignum's sawmill operation had loaded

Leonard Billy (on the right) helps adjust the horse harness.

trucks going out to Williams Lake and driving through our property every day! He could flag an empty one and get to our ranch any day he wanted.

But it didn't happen.

After waiting for two weeks, Alf and I drove to Alexis Creek to get him.

Leonard Billy was a cowboy, a big-game guide and a mechanic. In short, he was an all-around hand at any and all ranch doings. We were so fortunate to have met him, and that he was happy to work with us.

As a boy, he and his father had worked for the Lee family east of Alexis Creek for years, which was a thorough education for the young Leonard. He soon became one of our family. After supper we would all relax together, enjoying Leonard's many exciting stories of his life's adventures. He and his wife, Teresa, lived beside Cheshi Creek in a cabin from the Lignum mill fire. We later moved it upstream to a pretty grove of pine and poplars across from our mill, where Leonard worked with Alf.

Alf and Leonard built a (vehicular) bridge across the creek so Leonard could walk or drive to their cabin for his lunch. Leonard and his wife had a radio that brought them the noon messages from Williams Lake, which was especially appreciated by the Chilcotin people without phones. Alf would sometimes accompany Leonard home to hear the messages while Teresa made delicious bannock and steaks from *mowich* (deer), and they often had their children and grandchildren there to visit.

He could handle all of the horse-drawn haying equipment, run the bulldozer and help Alf run the sawmill. He and his son, Peter, cut pines and built a lot of fences.

Leonard was also an exceptional packer. I had a mare that I seldom used. She was smart, trail-wise and gentle, but saddles just would roll off of her. We called her Slippery. But Leonard would ride her out, alone, to get a deer for Teresa. By afternoon he would come walking in with a four-point buck lashed to his riding saddle. How he even loaded it alone was a mystery. Teresa would tan mule deer skins and make beautiful gloves, moccasins and jackets from them.

## BBQ MOOSE RIBS

It was September of 1964 and Alf and I were expecting our first moose hunter of the season. With the help of the older boys, we had our hay at Skinner Meadow all into fenced stacks and the cattle rounded up and ready for Alf to truck the beef to market. Our younger boys were eight and five years old by then, and I had hired a nice, competent housekeeper/cook who had a young son of about nine. They were a delightful addition to our family. Our boys got along well, and the three of them did the chores together after school. Alex liked collecting the eggs from the chickens, and they also brought in wood and water.

Our moose-hunting party included Marty, who was twenty by then and learning to be a guide, and Leonard Billy. Leonard would guide the hunter so I could do the campfire cooking for all of us.

We set up our camp at Moose Meadows, a string of wild hay and willow brush meadows six miles east of our wilderness lake camp, which was eighteen miles from the home base. It was a two-day pack trip from the Circle X.

The hunter got a fine bull on the second day out, which Leonard cleaned, butchered and quartered, ready to pack out on horses on the third day. He and Marty hung the quarters high up on our strong lodgepole pine log and wedged and tied between two stout spruce trees in the cool shade.

Leonard decided he wanted campfire barbequed ribs, so I built up the campfire to have a six-foot-long bed of coals ready for the barbequing.

Leonard and Marty went out into the forest for two dry lodgepole pine trees, cleaned them both of any bark and measured them. One had to be eleven or twelve feet long and sharpened on both ends, and the other fifteen feet long and sharpened only on one end. The other end had a strong fork to act as a support to the first pole, which would hold the ribs.

Then Leonard and Marty skewered the first pole through one side of ribs, in and out, in and out, until the whole side was firmly attached to the pole.

The sharpened end was then impaled firmly into the ground at an angle to expose one side of the ribs to the hot coals. The second pole with the fork supported the meat pole with its V-crotch, and its sharp end was stuck in the ground.

As the day darkened, our camp became a pool of light in the black, embracing forest. Our three white tents caught the firelight, as did Leonard's and Marty's serious faces as they cut slivers of roasted moose meat to sample while they commented in low voices, crouching beside the glowing coals, as to whether it was time to swap the ends of the meat pole yet to roast the other side. The fat had been dripping oil onto the coals, which sizzled on contact, sending up a delicious aroma, and our hunter was busy snapping pictures.

Soon my vegetables were bubbling in their pots at the other end of the bed of coals. Our delicious dinner would soon be ready. I was thrilled that Leonard had introduced us to his method for roasting moose ribs without an oven.

## LIGNUM SAWMILL

In 1964, when the Lignum Sawmill moved into the valley to set up their mill beside Tatlayoko Lake, my two oldest boys went to work for them, along with other local men. Lignum started building skid roads throughout our virgin fir-timbered valley. For starters they laid their logging road onto our hand-cut and hand-maintained cattle trail. Alf had to bulldoze a new trail up the hillside and put block salt on it to wean the cattle away from the thirty-five-year-old cattle trail. Since we salted them on the original trail, they always lay around on it to chew their cud. We could find them there when we rode on horseback to check on them, so we named their gathering place "Cow Town."

## KEVAN'S 4-H CALF

In 1965, the year Kevan turned nine, a neighbour organized a 4-H Calf program for kids in our community. Alf and I asked Kevan if he would like to join. We told him that we would help him pick out a good Hereford steer calf from our herd; then he would be

The Lignum Sawmill was built in 1964. Both Marty and Barry worked there until it burned down.

responsible for feeding it, grooming it, teaching it to lead and writing a daily report of all of this to take to the meetings with the other children.

"Then what?" Kevan wanted to know.

"Then next fall, when he's a year and a half old, we take you and your steer to the 4-H show in Williams Lake where all the calves will be judged. You could win first prize if you work hard at it." I explained that the calves were then auctioned off and the first-prize calf always brought the most money, because it was usually bought by a town businessman who supported the 4-H clubs. Also, the winner would get his picture in the local paper beside his calf.

"Who gets the money?" our fledging businessman demanded.

"You do," I said. "It's your calf. So how about it?"

"Okay," Kevan agreed.

We went out to the pen where our calves were being fed before being trucked to the sale. Together, the three of us decided on a sturdy, well-marked, typical Hereford steer calf. He had a white face, mane and brisket, white feet and white at the end of his tail.

We separated him from the others and instructed Kevan to give him an armful of good clover hay so the calf could get used to him. The calf had access to the creek and the barn for shelter.

The routine was good for Kevan. Soon the calf, whom Kevan had named Hercules, was gentle enough to brush and comb. I suggested putting a halter on him to teach him to lead. For starters, Kevan tied him to the sturdy manger, which taught the calf not to pull back.

Alf and I learned a lot too, especially about Kevan. He was no quitter; he fed his calf before and after school, gave him grain once every day, offered him a salt block to lick, and allowed him to run loose in a six-acre pasture connected to the barnyard. Soon he would come to Kevan's call and allowed himself to be led. Hercules was growing fast, and he went into winter with a thick coat of Hereford-red hair.

When the kids attended their meetings, they exchanged ideas. Most of them kept their calves in a building or small pen with a shed roof in one corner.

But not Kevan. Hercules slept in the barn, but spent a big part of his days roaming around the pasture. Kevan's explanation was that his calf was building muscle, as one side of the pasture was steep.

Fall arrived and the cattle sales were looming, including the 4-H sales.

Kevan and I led his whopping nine-hundred-pound "calf" into our pickup to drive to Williams Lake. On the way we had a flat tire. We got the spare and jacked the truck up to exchange it. Hercules was annoyed at the slope of the deck and began kicking the side of the box. Kevan scratched and consoled the hulk while I hurriedly changed the tire before he could break out and escape.

At the stockyards we couldn't unload him because the chute we backed up to was for bigger trucks than our pickup, and it was so dark we couldn't find a lower one. We decided to leave the steer in the truck overnight, so we drove out to Uncle Walter's place, where we were staying. He welcomed us and showed us where to park the pickup so it would be level. After we fed and watered Kevan's steer, we had some supper and Walter provided beds for our exhausted bodies.

The next morning, after breakfast, we drove back to the stockyards to unload Hercules. We saw a manure pile we could back up to with a big telephone pole alongside. I got the rope, attached it to the steer's halter shank and wrapped it a couple of times around the pole. With Kevan hanging onto the rope, I took down the end gate so Hercules could step out onto the handy manure pile.

But he didn't step out. He bolted out! The rope went ringing around the pole and Kevan couldn't hold on. The steer was terrified by all the noise and traffic, and he took off into the lakeside traffic at a gallop, dragging the rope.

We were all sure he was going to cause a wreck or at least break a leg. We gave chase on foot. Some kind soul stopped the steer, turned him and helped us chase him in among some pens where we cornered him and tied him solidly.

Then I went for our pickup. We tied him to the ball hitch, then drove to the 4-H barn where he was stabled, in the company of other 4-H animals. He'd had his run, so thankfully he behaved.

Kevan and I heaved a sigh of relief. The show and sale were two days away. Kevan would feed, water and wash Hercules as the other 4-H kids were doing, tying their animals outside to a sturdy fence to hose and groom them.

For the next two days Kevan almost lived with his steer. When Hercules lay down to chew his cud, Kevan would curl up in the clean hay beside him. They became very close. Hercules was like a pet, and he had absolute trust in Kevan. It would be hard for Kevan to give him up.

Soon the fateful day was at hand. The 4-H kids led their animals into the show ring for the judge to evaluate them and record their best points. Sure enough, Hercules ranked close to the top for muscle tone, and he sold to my nine-year-old rancher-in-training for nine hundred dollars.

## THE FIGHT FOR A BIGGER, BETTER SCHOOL

The first school in Tatlayoko Valley was a one-room log building built by the young, strong fathers of the landed half-dozen families living in the valley in the early 1930s. Ten children were required to open a school, and a family living in Nemiah Valley, where there was no school, moved to Tatlayoko Valley. Their children then brought the numbers up, so the school was granted.

KB had loaned a cabin of his own to be used as a schoolroom until the log building was completed. Most of those families settled near the Circle X Ranch, so the location for the school was at that end of the valley near the north end of Tatlayoko Lake.

As those children were graduating out of grade eight and more families moved in further up the valley, the log school was moved nearer to them. In 1951, Marty was seven years old, and we drove the kids to the school in the new pickup truck Grandpa had bought.

However, the original road was made along the riverbank which, in March, was only drivable by tractor. I drove our Ford-Ferguson tractor six miles each way to take my two boys and a neighbour's three kids to school and then back home. The kids rode in a two-wheeled open trailer behind the tractor, and I covered them with a tarpaulin to protect them from the showers of mud thrown up by the large wheels of the tractor.

During the sixties the Williams Lake School District held a meeting for the eleven "unorganized" schools throughout the district. By this time, Lignum's Mill had moved into Tatlayoko Valley with its forty employees and their big families. They hastily built a lumber cookshack, but it became the school for their children.

The teachers at that time were an American couple, and the building was so crowded that the smaller children were crammed into the cloakroom. At that time I was the local correspondent to the *Tribune*. I knew about the impending annual school-board meeting in Williams Lake and I enquired if any local person would be going there to represent us.

No one stepped forward, so I took on the challenge. I took photos of the cookshack school congestion before leaving Tatlayoko

Valley. So far so good, but there was another piece necessary to complete the picture that I wished to present to the school board.

I drove to the mill to ask the Lignum's Mill manager and crew if they would build another schoolhouse—a larger one—so they could get their cookhouse back.

"Sure thing!" they said. "We're getting rent for our cookhouse. Why not build a school and rent that?"

I drove to Williams Lake to attend the school-board meeting. There were ten men representing ten Chilcotin schools. We were cordially received and introduced to the board members seated around a huge mahogany oval table. We sat in chairs lined up along the wall for fifteen minutes while they conducted school-board business, and then we were invited into a small office with only one visitor's chair at the desk.

A gentleman stood behind his desk, both hands flat on it. He scanned the room, full of dissatisfied male parents, and asked, "Who would like to go first?"

No one spoke up. So I said: "If no one else is ready, I am."

"Okay, let's hear it," he said, still standing.

I addressed him politely by name, then asked him if he was satisfied with the "instant schoolhouse" the Lignum's Mill people had built at Tatlayoko Lake.

"Oh yes," he replied, "it's a fine building, well lit and well attended."

I spread my photos on his desk and said: "I'm glad to hear you say that, Sir, because we are prepared to build another one just like it, only larger."

He sat down, seemed like he was thinking about this, and then asked me to go home, draw up a plan for a school and submit it to him.

I left the room to the rest of those who had problems to discuss.

I went out and purchased a package of various coloured craft sheets and several sheets of lined graph paper to take home with me. With the graph paper and a survey of our valley's deeded lands, I began enlarging the seven-inch authentic map of the settled part of the valley onto an eighteen-inch sheet of graph paper. First I painstakingly drew in the Homathko River, then the road, the deeded lots with lot numbers and the owners' surnames, then the two schools.

To show the population of children I punched circles from the craft paper: pale green for preschoolers; dark green for kids in grades one to seven; yellow for grade eight and, though we didn't have it but needed it, orange for grade nine and red for grade ten.

When the official saw my map he was impressed. He could see with a glance at the coloured spots aligned at each home that the older children were grouped at one end of the valley and the lesser grades at the other.

My suggestion was to split the grades into two groups, making it easier for the single teachers, and less driving for the parents. I also requested that our teenage students be given a teacher for grades nine and ten, so they would at least qualify for training in various trades for which grade ten was required.

The Williams Lake School Board came through handsomely. We had a new school built in the valley to accommodate all of the valley children, including grades nine and ten, and a capable and

The original school in Tatlayoko became so crowded in the sixties that I started to campaign for a new school. Eventually the Wllliams Lake School Board came through with some funding and a modern new school was built.

strict principal was hired. The lower grades were shared by two teachers and there were separate classrooms, a health room for children who weren't feeling well and a library.

We were given a school bus for all the valley kids, and from our ranch the six miles were now a ten-minute ride, with no more slow trips by tractor. Children from further away boarded with Tatlayoko Valley neighbours during the week.

We were delighted with our modern school. Our three teachers had separate but adjoining apartments just seventy yards away from the school.

Soon our school became the community centre for our valley. We held social evenings, which provided entertainment for everyone: dart games in one room and dancing in two rooms (modern and square dancing), and the library was designated for poker players. Movie nights were also popular. Everyone brought potluck food and deposited it on a big table in the hallway. It was wonderful.

# Potato Mountain Cabins

With our summer cattle range on the south end of Potato Mountain, our guide-outfitting and trail-riding business included mountain rides to check the cattle. I had always dreamed of building a cabin on Potato Mountain as a shelter for our range riding, trail riders and hunters, as well as a place to safely store our supplies and camp gear. We could never leave anything up there on the mountain because of the bears. They had already destroyed two of my camps when I had just left them overnight with groceries hanging in pack boxes from a high pole.

## Our First Cabin from Whitebark Pines

In July of 1972, my oldest son, Marty, his girlfriend, Aleta, and I started building a range cabin on the south end of Potato Mountain. It was our first log-cabin-building effort on Potato Mountain, and we learned a lot.

We found an ideal location up near the top of the mountain on a flat four-acre meadow surrounded by trees. It was just the right size for a cabin, and the open grazing land was only a half mile away.

The view from there was spectacular. To the south and east, the ten-thousand-foot Coast Range peaks decorated the horizon. Outside the fringe of sheltering trees was an open hillside with scattered clumps of whitebark pine and balsamroot for horse feed.

One of the best things about this site was the spring, about eighty yards up the hill, so we could run water to the cabin.

Our pack horse, Uncle Bulgy, packed our tools, food, tent and sleeping bags up the mountain. Once we picked out the straightest trees, felled and limbed them, we got Uncle Bulgy to drag the green logs in for us. We peeled them and set the bottom logs for the new cabin on flat rocks to prevent rot. By six o'clock we had two rounds done on the eight-by-twelve-foot cabin. Time to quit and make supper and stake and hobble the horses for the night.

The cabin building continued for the next five days without a hitch—except for something we hadn't counted on. No matter how carefully we chose our cabin logs, they didn't look too good once they were horizontal and notched together, and our four walls ended up with gaping holes all around. These whitebark pine trees were not lodgepole pines, which are straight and taper gradually so they fit snugly together. Unfortunately, lodgepole pines didn't grow at this elevation. Whitebark pines are pitchy, limby and crooked and, it turned out, not good cabin-building material. Their butts are

We learned the hard way that whitebark pine logs are not straight enough for cabin walls. But it wasn't so bad—at least the cabin was airy and bright.

wide and their tops are very narrow. Our cabin was going to let the breeze in and would definitely be a summertime shelter.

Oh well—we could only do our best with what we had. On the bright side, there was no need for windows because you could look out the gaps between the logs to see who was riding up, and the holes let plenty of light in.

In five days we had the walls up, and the stringers and ridgepole were in place for the roof. We could throw a tarp over the frame if it threatened rain, at least until we could get some roofing up to it. We were hoping to use milled boards.

Marty made a note of what we needed to bring on our next trip up the mountain: blasting powder to blow the sludge out of the spring, a garden hose to bring the water down the hill to our cabin and some short boards and nails to build a water trough for the horses.

A week or so later we brought up the powder to blow the spring. I stood out in the open to photograph the action, but when the charge went off and boulders were lofted skyward, I ran behind a tree for cover before they crashed right where I had been standing.

The spring was cleared and the water was cold and sweet. We brought the water close to the cabin with a garden hose, as the spring was conveniently uphill. We built a three-foot-long trough for the horses and filled it with the hose, and then we fenced the spring with big logs so no horse or cow or wildlife would drop into the six-foot-deep well. The animals on the range could all drink their fill from the creek four hundred yards away.

We discussed what this project had taught us while we sat around the campfire. For one thing, we had learned to never use any trees other than lodgepole pines for cabin building! These whitebark pines were handy and good enough for shelter, but they were no good for building the proper guest cabin that our summertime guests and hunters would require.

Our new neighbours eventually solved the problem of the roof. We had told them they were welcome to use the cabin, and when they hired a helicopter to search for scattered cattle, they also flew in some roofing. Despite the gaps in its walls, the finished cabin came in handy for emergency shelter and storing camp gear and extra salt for the horses and cattle.

## ALEX'S WILDERNESS WEEKEND

By 1974 Marty had his own ranch about fifteen miles away in the mountainous wilderness south of Tatlayoko Lake. He called it "God's Pocket." At that time Alex was fifteen and was attending high school in Williams Lake. He would come home by school bus on Fridays and Alf would drive to Tatla to collect him and bring him home.

Alex was always happy to be home. One Saturday morning we loaded his horse, Cricket, onto our son Barry's pickup along with

Alex looked forward to coming home on the weekends. He was a natural hunter and cowboy.

some extra food and left for Marty's ranch. Our plan for the weekend was to hew out a trail from Marty's homestead up and over the mountain range to the next valley, where the mighty Stikelan Creek runs from glaciers up at its headwaters. It picks up the water from other creeks to become Big Creek, as we call it locally, as it enters Tatlayoko Lake.

Marty and his girlfriend, Aleta, were glad to see us, and she had a fine meal ready. She and Marty were putting a roof onto their porch.

We had some of our horses pastured at Marty's place, and

Alex and me in front of the Circle X Ranch house, with one of our regular hunters, Dr. Diehl.

Flying to Williams Lake for Kevan's high school rodeo.

Aleta, Marty and Alex went into the bush to find some horses for us to ride. I had my horse Joe staked out and available.

We packed one horse and rode up to hunt out Rafferty's Trail, which was made in 1928 by Al Rafferty to join onto the BC surveyors' trail. The undergrowth had grown up so thick that Marty had to unlimber his chainsaw, and both Marty and Alex hewed their way up the mountain with Marty's power saw growling and Alex's machete swinging. Aleta and I cleared the brambles and rocks off the trail and led the horses along.

Moose and deer beds were vacated by the animals startled by our commotion, but they would greatly enjoy that trail, now free of branches and rocks. The antlered animals always prefer a cleared trail to limby forests.

The men kept losing the beautifully graded Rafferty trail, and we finally gave up on it and climbed straight up as dark was coming on. We needed water and grass for the horses. For fifteen minutes we struggled through thick timber and big boulders. I bet Alex five dollars we would come out on a lake.

Sure enough, we came out on a nice little grassy meadow beside a small lake and unpacked and unsaddled our tired horses so they could drink and graze. Then we built a campfire. The moon was pretty full so we could easily see to make camp. What a beautiful campsite! We had our stew pot bubbling in nothing flat while our horses munched happily on the lush grass.

We rolled out our sleeping bags and crawled in. There was a light snow falling onto our tents, which didn't last. The next morning, early, Alex and Marty restaked the horses while Aleta and I cooked breakfast. We were delighted with the lake. When we climbed a little hill to see all of it, we found it was shaped like a clover leaf, so we named it Good Luck Lake.

Continuing on, we found the surveyor trail again, with five-inch birch and Russian poplar growing in the middle of it. We followed it through the pass between Lone Mountain and Rafferty's Basin mine camp, where I found an undamaged quart jar with "1935" embossed on the bottom. I still have it.

Signs of Rafferty's pioneer tent camp were still there, and

the rotting-down sidewalls of five-inch poles were still in position. Pole walls give height (headspace) to a tent. Rafferty had cleared a twenty-foot-long path through a rock slide, which was still clean and perfect. It was pack-horse wide and five feet in depth. No new slides had come down from 1934 to now.

We found a one-acre meadow, which we named Threshold Meadow, right at the edge of Stikelan Creek. We found that the surveyors had made a camp there and had carved "B.C. Surveyors 1928" into a still-living tree. It was a perfect campsite with a small creek, so we unpacked and spent the night.

The next morning, we rode alongside Stikelan Creek past the canyon until we found a good crossing. The water was low, so we crossed easily and joined our regular horse trail for home. We could feel the horses' relief at this turn of direction. It was like, "Let's go home! It's all downhill from here!"

We arrived home by 3:00 p.m., stripped the saddles and packs off the horses and turned them loose to roll and graze. Supper was a joyful event as we recounted our adventures to the others, especially when we told them about the sign carved into the tree by the surveyors back in 1928. We had enjoyed reopening that old trail, connecting Copper Creek Valley to Stikelan Valley through the wilderness.

## THE SECOND POTATO MOUNTAIN CABIN AT ECHO LAKE

We still needed a range cabin and a shelter for our trail-riding and hunting guests on the south end of Potato Mountain. This time we were determined to build it with lodgepole pine. Ideally we wanted the cabin beside a lake, with a stand of fire-killed trees nearby for firewood. I wanted something quite roomy with a loft to hold plenty of people.

We discovered an ideal location right on Echo Lake, which had the added benefit of early-morning sun. I named it Echo Lake because my yodeling came back to me sharp and clear from the steeply rising hillside on the other side of the lake. The only thing missing was a stand of lodgepole pine, but they never grow at that elevation.

On the way down the mountain the next day we paid more attention, watching for a nice, evenly aged stand of lodgepole pine. We found one right on our mountain trail, almost two miles from the end of Echo Lake, and began laying plans for our next and better mountain cabin ... whooooeee!

In July 1974, Alex, Leonard Billy and Marty started cutting logs for the Echo Lake cabin. It took all summer to cut and haul the logs two miles up the trail to the cabin site. The boys did everything by hand, using one old horse to drag the logs to the lake. Then they rafted them to the other end of the lake, using paddles and a tarp as a sail to catch the prevailing wind to propel them.

We built the cabin the following summer. Leonard was the expert who knew how to do it. We were on a gentle slope and he said we needed a level to lay the bottom logs properly. We didn't have one in our tool supply and it would have meant losing two days to ride back to the ranch to get one. Then I had an idea. I went to where our guests always threw their bottles when they were done with them and found a square, clear whisky bottle and filled

We built a sturdy lodgepole cabin on this lake, which I named Echo Lake.

Leonard Billy was an excellent carpenter and helped us build this lumber addition to the mini-lodge on Wilderness Lake.

it half-full of water. We had our level, and Leonard had a big smile on his face.

Work progressed, and once we got the cabin head-high, I got them to use longer logs to project over the front so we could have an upstairs bedroom loft over a covered porch. They were working on the roof when Leonard Billy spotted what he thought looked like a UFO. Alex was so excited he ran right off the top of the cabin to grab the binoculars before it flew away. Fortunately, at sixteen years old he was young and agile.

We later packed milled boards on our horses from Alf's saw-mill to finish off the roof and floor.

## LEASE-TO-PURCHASE LOT 230

In 1975 Alf applied for a ten-year lease with an option to purchase on the flood plain I had discovered while guiding moose hunters near Wilderness Lake. This lease, which later became Lot 230, was just beyond our cattle trail up the south end of Potato Mountain and on our hunting trail into Stikelan Valley.

It was a horrible piece of ground, all blowdowns and washouts. There were no standing trees because a fire had gone through it. I had to get across this gall-darn quarter mile of flood plain with the horses over five channels of Cheshi Creek. Then I looked down and saw a healthy clump of clover. I told Alf about it, and then he came and checked it out. He applied for the lease and that's how we got it.

We had a hunting camp on Wilderness Lake, which was halfway to Moose Meadows in the headwaters of Stikelan Creek and the pass over to Big Lagoon on Chilko Lake. Taking hunters by horseback into Moose Meadows was a two-day trip, and Wilderness Lake was the halfway point and the natural place to put our camp.

In 1969 we had obtained a permit for a five-acre satellite camp at Wilderness Lake and hired Henry Case, a Tsilhqot'in man from Redstone, to build us a log cabin there. He and his family camped next to the lake all summer but never finished the sixteen-by-eighteen-foot cabin. The stout walls were eight feet high but it still had no roof. Six years later the logs were turning grey.

The Stikelan Valley.

# SELLING THE CIRCLE X RANCH

In the spring of 1976, the Lignum Sawmill on Tatlayoko Lake burned to the ground. Since it had opened in 1964, the mill had siphoned off all the good help for ranchers—ranching just couldn't compete with the wages. Our older boys, Marty and Barry, and all the young people in the valley went to work in the mill and we didn't have any help on the ranch. They lived in a bunkhouse and worked every day. After ten days on the job they got four days off.

Marty and Barry had left the ranch to run their own lives, and when the mill burned down, they both lost their jobs. They couldn't stay in Tatlayoko without logging jobs, so they hired on with a logging company near Williams Lake.

Alf was never a complainer, but when he said we had to sell the ranch because he couldn't lift another bale, I agreed. My health was breaking down too. We were working too hard.

We had the first baler in the country. It was a stationary type that you had to bring the hay to, then fork it into the hopper to be baled. It produced six-hundred-pound bales tied with wire, about four feet long, three feet wide and a foot deep. We didn't have any equipment and had to handle all those bales by hand, picking them up and lifting them onto the wagon.

In October we sold the Circle X Ranch to Hans Schluter, a wheeler-dealer from Germany. We offered to stay the winter to teach him how to run the ranch and look after the cows, but he refused our offer and became very nasty. He said, "I want you out of here

189

in thirty days." He had suddenly transformed from the pleasant, glad-handing man we sold the ranch to.

Schluter paid us $380,000 and withheld $20,000 until we put our equipment "into running condition" the following spring. We had done all the haying and irrigating with it, so our bookkeeper suggested that we add the clause "according to its age," which we did.

But neither the equipment nor the cattle meant anything to Schluter. He let our handsome herd of Herefords die for lack of feed all winter long, even though there was plenty of hay. I'd drive by and it would break my heart seeing our cattle starving to death when we had all those sheds and stacks full of hay. Then in the spring he refused the final payment for the equipment.

His holdback of twenty thousand dollars was just a ruse. I got a lawyer and we went to court in Vancouver. The judge split that twenty thousand between us, and our lawyer got our ten thousand.

The machinery? Schluter bought new stuff. I should have said, "You keep your twenty thousand and we'll keep our 'worn-out,' 'broken-down' equipment." Alf and the boys had worked on it all winter, adding new parts. They even bought another tractor for him too.

Schluter turned out to be less than forthright, but he finally paid his dues. A few years later he died of double kidney failure despite having his own dialysis machines at our ranch and at the Graham Ranch in Tatla Lake, which he had also purchased. He had a similar story with the Grahams. He gave them the down payment and nothing else. We Canadians were too trusting.

When we sold the Circle X Ranch, Barry was living on the Marion place, about five miles up the valley from the ranch. I had traded the 160-acre Marion place to him for his inherited share of Skinner Meadow when we were still ranching. We couldn't ranch without that thousand-acre wild-grass meadow because it gave us the hay base we required.

With the money we got from the sale of the Circle X Ranch, I purchased three privately owned lots on the east bank of the Fraser River near Williams Lake. My plan was for it to be our retirement property since Alf and I were both suffering from exhaustion.

Thanks to a tip from our accountant, Betty, our health was restored by springtime. She suggested a daily dose of one capsule of vitamin E and one teaspoon of cod-liver oil, taken one hour before breakfast. We are forever thankful to Betty for suggesting this. Once we regained our health we were not ready for retirement.

## LOOKING FOR A HOME

Now homeless, in the fall of 1976, we rented the Olrich place for the winter. The Olriches had returned to the States after spending a few years in the old John Haynes shack they had bought along the Homathko River, three miles up the valley from the Circle X Ranch.

We stored our household effects in a mill shack I had bought from Barry for $150 that was parked in his field at the Marion place. It was one of nine lumber shacks Barry had purchased for eight hundred dollars from P&T Sawmill Company when their mill burned up at Chilanko Forks in 1974.

On April 1, 1977, All Fools' Day, our deal with Schluter was finally over. No matter. We had new fish to fry.

In June, no longer ranching and with our health restored, Alf and I moved to Wilderness Lake. We finally had time to put a roof on the Henry Case cabin, and Alf started clearing Lot 230.

The campsite was a jungle of windfalls when we arrived to pitch our leaky Pioneer tent on the west shore of Wilderness Lake. Barry strode in with his chainsaw, and within two hours he had bucked that jungle into a clearing. Under my instruction, he built a "Chilcotin cooker"—a waist-high four-foot-square log crib filled with rocks and gravel on which I could build my camp cooking fire. No more bending over for me, and I could hang my pots and frying pans on its sides. A firewood pile appeared suddenly beside it.

Barry cut some windfalls into various lengths to become a useful vertical kitchen wall, with a table against it and nails to hang utensils from. To pretty up my kitchen I placed potted geraniums on the flattened tops of the upright logs. My kitchen wall varied in height but was roughly five feet high.

Our large Pioneer tent was then erected at right angles to the kitchen on a board floor. Alf's and my bed along with my Singer sewing machine were moved into the tent, and this became our 1977 summer home.

To add more charm to this lakeside camp, Alex, now graduated from high school, brought me a bunch of flat flagstones about two feet square for my yard. He found this outcropping of rocks across the lake, standing like a rock wall, and he built a three-sided sauna against it, with a heater, floor and roof. It was beside deep water too, so it was a very charming bathhouse, even for future guests. Alex hauled several loads of these flat rocks to my camp on his raft. My table was a large wooden telephone-wire spool, centred in the yard on the patio of flat rocks with chairs all around.

Within two or three hours we had a cozy, useful, charming home to shelter us and work out of. It felt a bit like a fairy tale, and we even had three loons who would parade by on the lake, one by one.

We'd had no time to finish the Henry Case cabin while we were still ranching. Now Alf used his Cat to align the log structure with the lake, so our picture window over the table gave a lovely view of the lake, mountains and forests. It was only twenty feet from the water.

I asked Alf to please build a loft in the cabin, similar to our cabin at Echo Lake, which would double the sleeping space. He increased the height of the walls by an extra six rounds of logs and made the upper logs seven feet longer than those used by Henry Case. The front of the cabin jutted out, providing an overhanging roof for the outside porch. Upstairs we had plenty of space in the loft for a double bed.

We enjoyed a lovely summer with no rain, so we stayed dry even though our tent leaked. The night we moved into the Henry Case cabin, the sky opened up and rain poured down. I lay blissfully listening to it pounding on our roof, revelling in the luxury and marvelling at the wisdom and determination of my husband. What a man! What an exciting, wonderful life we were living! We didn't miss the ranch or cows by then.

We called the Henry Case cabin our mini-lodge, and I so enjoyed it. I could cook meals on the wood cookstove and serve the meals on the big dining table beside the four-foot-square window with a magnificent view of the lake and surrounding hills and mountains. On a calm morning there would be mirror-image reflections on the lake.

Several years later, Leonard Billy and I added another room to the side of our mini-lodge, built out of lumber. It gave us space for a double bed and pantry shelves. Three windows and a door to the outside made it very sunny and delightful, and the back door allowed for an easier exit. Two outhouses, a men's and a ladies', were discreetly situated up the hill facing the forest, and a large woodshed was added as well.

Several hundred people have now enjoyed this dear, homey lakeshore cabin since it was built, including groups of Boy Scouts and school kids and parties of tourists. I guided summer guests and fall hunters from it for several years, and some guests prefer it to the main lodge even now.

Alex helped Alf and Leonard clear the new land for the lease. At eighteen years old, Alex was running the Cat. As they cleared off the timber, they used the pine rails to fence the pasture, and the bigger logs went through Alf's new sawmill for timbers, railway ties and lumber.

## THE LANE CABIN

With fall coming on we had to do something about a winter residence for ourselves, preferably with power and on a road that got snowploughed regularly.

Though Skinner Meadow was sold with the ranch, Alf still owned a lease-to-purchase lot right next to it on Skinner Lake, and we still owned the Skinner Meadow access road that left the main Tatlayoko Road across from the Marion place. Why not skid our $150 fire-sale cabin from Barry's field and set it next to our access road?

Power had recently come to Tatlayoko Valley, and a branch line had marched up our access road to neighbours living way up on Skinner Mountain. So we moved our cabin next to the access road, had a lineman drop a power line into the cabin only thirty feet

We moved this $150 fire-sale cabin to the Skinner Meadow access road. The Lane Cabin became our home for the winter of 1977.

from a pole, and furnished the cabin to make it cozy and homey for the winter.

It was not possible to stay on Lot 230 over the winter because we would be snowed in, so by November 30, when hunting season was over, we moved into the lane cabin and brought our thirty horses up valley to winter on Alf's lease at Skinner Lake.

There they could rustle until January and then we would bring them home to the Marion place to be fed hay every day until May. When the grass started growing in the spring, we would bring them back to Lot 230 and their unfenced range at Wilderness Lake.

## Trading Properties with the Boys

That winter I traded our lots near the Fraser to Barry and Marty in exchange for the return of my two Tatlayoko Valley properties, the Marion place and the Puckett place. I gave them both extra cash to balance the values of lots versus acreage. They were happy to be only eight miles from Williams Like with guaranteed jobs, and they still are.

Our obliging notary public was in a spin trying to keep all of our land tradings with our sons legal and straight!

## A BULL BEFORE BREAKFAST

My first bull moose hunt in the fall of 1977 got off to a good start. We had nice clients, nice weather and our newly completed three-room mini-lodge to work out of on the shore of Wilderness Lake.

The three hunters, Jim, Fred and Bob, had arrived the evening before. They had rested well and as I poured their morning coffee, I asked if they might like a little stroll while waiting for breakfast. I told them about the natural mineral seepage on the shore of Wilderness Lake about a quarter mile away, where deer and moose would come to lick the wet mud for minerals.

I suggested that one fellow take the canoe over to the lick to check for moose tracks, while the other two walked around the lake from the cabin on our horse trail. I told them breakfast would be ready in a half hour.

Jim got into the canoe and Bob and Fred were headed down the trail when I stopped them. "You ought to carry your rifles," I suggested. "The bulls are in the rut, and they can be dangerous."

They went for their rifles and left again. In fifteen minutes, a barrage of shooting rent the quiet morning. I kept on with the breakfast, smiling to myself, thinking they had been sighting in their rifles. Soon I heard the sound of someone running to the cabin. Bob was all out of breath. "Come quick," he said. "We've got a bull moose down; it's dead and we don't know what to do now!"

Alex was scheduled to arrive by noon to assist me, and I was wishing he was here now. I put the breakfast into the warming oven, grabbed my hunting knife and followed Bob up the trail.

Sure enough, a big bull lay in a low depression alongside the trail. I set to open him up, while two men held his hind legs apart. It was impossible to bleed him while he lay in the shallow ditch, and he was too heavy for us to drag onto level ground. I just had to wait for the blood to coagulate, which it did shortly.

Once the blood thickened to the consistency of liver, I began scooping it out in great chunks and chucking it off to one side. Unfortunately I had left the cabin without grabbing the axe from the woodpile. This would have allowed me to chop open the sternum to better remove the heart, liver, windpipe and lungs. As the rib cage of a moose resembles a horse, I had to reach further and further up inside to thoroughly bleed the cavity. My arms were bloody to my shoulder and my white shirt was now red. I rolled all the innards onto the ground and dragged them away, then propped the cavity open with strong sticks to cool down the body.

We had definitely worked up an appetite for breakfast as we headed back to the cabin at the other end of the lake. Thank goodness the lake was right near the cabin door so I could wash up! A clean shirt restored my housewifely image. We sat down to our put-on-hold breakfast with a great deal of satisfaction.

After we had eaten, Alex showed up in time to help us. He was surprised we already had a moose. While he went for our little red tractor over at the fence-building project, the hunters and I walked down to quarter the moose.

The men all helped load the quarters onto the box behind the tractor. Then Alex hauled it to the stout meat-hanging log high up in a grove of spruce. It was an ideal place to hang meat: shaded, with a cool breeze coming off the lake.

Alex caught and saddled five horses while I made pocket lunches. We mounted up for their first day's hunt into the roadless wilderness. Our destination was Moose Meadows, a swampy area between two mountain ranges, six miles away.

The horse trail took us right there, where we could rest and graze our horses and eat our lunches while glassing the Bracewell Mountains for wildlife. There were a number of unnamed peaks in the Coast Mountains south of Potato Mountain, and we had selected a range in honour of Alf, but it couldn't be gazetted until after he had died.

We would be hunting this area on foot so we unbridled and unsaddled our horses. The horses enjoyed a good roll and drink at the creek before grazing. Now we could stake some and hobble the others to be sure they'd be there on our return.

We had come around seven-thousand-foot Marmot Mountain during our ride. That south side was rocky with some brush, and we glassed it for bears searching for berries. Then we turned our binoculars on the Alf Bracewell Mountains to the south, ideal for mountain goats, especially billies, who keep cooler on the north side facing us.

We were rewarded by seeing two billy goats, one smaller than the other, probably three-year-olds. Leaving our lucky moose hunter, Bob, to enjoy the goats and keep the horses company, we separated to cover more area and also so we would be quieter. Jim and I went north toward an old beaver dam to scout from a ridge, while Alex and his hunter, Fred, went into the spruce forest to the south. There were little grassy openings and lots of red willows among the spruce trees.

Jim and I hiked through stunted willows that had been heavily browsed by moose to intercept my little ridge. It lay north to south and led right to the beaver dam. The ridge was only six feet wide, but it afforded an open view of the spruce and pine forest that covered the flanks of Bracewell Mountain up to the bare rocks. A little one-acre meadow was right below us.

"We'll just stop here awhile and listen," I quietly told Jim. The faint breeze had a hint of fall to it. Willow and poplar leaves were rust and golden coloured; a bald eagle soared above us. There was no sound of anything. It was such a beautiful fall day.

I gave a low bull-moose grunt, looking up the mountainside at the new forest of young pine. I knew from experience that rotting windfalls from a fire fifty years earlier littered the forest floor. Where there's been a fire there are fire willows—the favourite food of moose. They could be in that jungle.

Suddenly there was a crash on the hillside above us, then silence. Three long minutes later I grunted again, and the crashes came closer.

"Get a shell into your chamber, Jim, and put the safety on," I whispered. "I'll try to call him down out of the forest, so be ready."

Minutes later, with no further response, I grunted softly again. Moose have very big ears, and they can move silently through anything. This time a twig snapped. The bull was closer now, just above the meadow. We waited, tense and silent, hiding in the shade of a pine to help shield our presence.

"Here he comes," I whispered as the tops of some small pines shook on the brushy rim of the meadow. Then a moose stepped right out into that small meadow: a fine, big, fully grown cow moose with no antlers. But she had the gleam of love in her eyes!

Jim and I stood rooted in surprise and disappointment.

"I thought you were a bull," I said to her.

Her expectant look answered back to me, "I thought *you* were a bull!"

She turned and, in two strides, disappeared into the thick green forest. We relaxed then and laughed at the trick she had played on us. I was secretly pleased that my grunting could sound enough like a bull to call in a cow moose.

## OUR FIRST GROUP OF WINTER GUESTS, MARCH 1978

Once we had the Potato Mountain cabin built at Echo Lake, I did a bit of advertising over the winter for people who like alpine skiing in March. Potato Mountain boasts miles of open alpine meadows up to seven thousand feet in elevation. By late winter there would be an eight-foot snow base on Potato Mountain, accessible by hiking, skiing or snowmobiling our six miles of hand-groomed mountainside trail to the cabin. That good snow base was topped with a light dusting of powder.

Alf had snowploughed the valley road to our Wilderness Lake cabin for our guests, who would be a family of four with two little girls, ten and eight years old. They were scheduled to arrive in two weeks. They had planned to stay at our cozy, well-equipped Wilderness Lake mini-lodge, but the snowpack at that lower elevation was not as good as it was up at our mountain cabin.

On the day of their arrival, the Gallaso family came walking the last mile to the mini-lodge after driving to the end of Alf's ploughed road. We became a very congenial group, eating and visiting together. Marty and Alex joined us as well as our nephew Gordy, his wife, Judy, and their son, David. That night we bedded nine people in the cabin—with two beds to spare!

The next morning Marty was up at 6:00 a.m. making hotcakes while Alex played Gordy's guitar from up on his bed in the loft.

After breakfast I baked the bread, which had been rising all night. Ten loaves for ten people!

While the Gallaso family skied on the deeply frozen Wilderness Lake, I packed supplies to be ready if our guests were up to making their assault on Potato Mountain. When they returned from skiing the half-mile lake all rosy cheeked and energized, we sat down with a round of coffee to make them aware of the pioneering aspects of skiing our Potato Mountain paradise. The cabin had no door or windows yet, and there was no chinking between the logs, but our lodgepole pine logs fit snugly.

Accessing the cabin meant crawling in under the bottom log, three feet off the ground. We would pitch our tents inside and have our evening heating and cooking campfire on the dirt floor. They decided to chance it.

Marty, Gordy, Judy and David had come with three snowmobiles to take part in the activities. They became our freighters, hauling food, gear and me up to the mountain cabin on that clear, beautiful March morning. Alex took a load with his snowmobile as well.

I wanted to prepare the cabin and have firewood split and ready for their arrival, so I went ahead. I spread a tarpaulin on the bare ground under the bottom log so I could wrassle the tent and a tied bundle of firewood inside. There had been some floor planks left over from the roofing job, and Alex and Leonard had covered a quarter of the floor space with them, spiking them down to the floor joists.

I set up the tent on the plank floor, placing my foamy and sleeping bag off to one side. There was a loft with a ladder and plenty of floor space up there for the men, but Gordy, Judy and David slept outside in igloos they dug out of the snowbank. They made a ledge for their beds, a cooking ledge and a candle shelf, and they used a tarp for the door.

Don Shelley, a neighbour from Tatlayoko, hiked up and established his tent camp on a ledge above the cabin. So there we were, three households on the mountaintop!

Diane Gallaso had brought daffodils from her own garden, which she carried with her as she and the children skied up the snowmobile trail. They took their time, since they were from sea-level country.

By three o'clock everyone was present and accounted for, and there was a surprise for everyone at the cabin! Although the snow around the cabin was eight feet deep, there was none in front of the cabin entrance. The fierce winter winds had sucked it all away, and the eight feet of packed winter snow stopped like a vertical wall six feet from the cabin. We cut steps down and hung a rope from the porch beams to get down and back up.

Although daylight lasts longer on a mountaintop, by the time I had a bed of coals to heat the hearty stew, everyone was ready to roll in under the bottom log and enjoy the cozy campfire. The fresh home-baked bread went well with the stew, and we had canned peaches for dessert. Everyone perched on the sturdy floor joists with the firelight reflecting off the walls. We traded lots of stories about the day's adventures, and then Diane put her willing young-sters into their sleeping bags beside hers on the partial floor. Their dad opted to sleep in the loft with Alex and Marty.

I took half of our vegetables to bed with me to prevent them from freezing, and Alex took the other half to his bed in the loft. We fell asleep to the crackle and glow of the small, dying fire as it flashed on the high ceiling of new lumber. Our day had been a great success, with our guests absorbing every facet of the raw wilder-ness that we had managed to tame just a little.

On our last day, the morning dawned sunny and calm for our descent. It had been a fantastic, fast-paced weekend. After a camp-fire breakfast, everyone packed up for the trail, heading down with skis or on foot. The snowmobilers hauled everyone's excess gear and most of the people down to the waiting vehicles. Judy and I hiked the steeper parts, carrying our skis and using our ski poles for balance. Occasionally we stopped so I could attend to my blis-tered heels. Ski boots are not made for hiking.

Judy collected a hatful of souvenirs such as pine cones, clumps of needles from various evergreens and different tree mosses. She saw moose tracks, squirrel tracks and rabbit tracks. Then Alex came roaring back to give us a welcome lift the last two miles home.

At the cabin I quickly heated a pot of chicken stew for our last meal together. Our guests praised us and paid Alex his well-earned wages. After everyone had left, I washed the dishes and cleaned up while Alex loaded our gear, including the daffodils, onto the sled. We sped quickly across the lake to our truck and returned to the valley with its bare fields, horses, robins and bawling cows.

## MORE IMPROVEMENTS TO WILDERNESS LAKE CAMP

As our tourism business thrived, Alf decided I needed a second cabin for guests rather than a tent, so that summer he and Leonard built me a nice single-room log cabin twenty feet from the mini-lodge. Like the mini-lodge it has a spectacular view of Alf Bracewell Mountain Range—so perfectly mirrored on the lake that it is hard to tell up from down.

The bunkhouse has two windows and holds four beds and a Selkirk heater. I bought double sliding-glass doors and installed them on the lake side, opening onto a roomy porch with a picnic table and benches. We still rent this hideaway now for groups of up to ten.

Wilderness Lake.

202

## CORRALS FOR THE HORSES AND COW

Our horses and milk cow needed a set of corrals to hold them, and we needed an enclosure in which to work the horses. That summer we made two corrals: one for hot days to give the horses the cooling breeze off the lake while being shaded by the surrounding trees, and a second yard on a sunny, grassy hillside for cooler weather.

We kept block salt in both corrals. When the horses came to their salt, we would hear their bells, and even after dark, we would go close the gate on them. Then we'd head happily back to bed, knowing there would be no horse hunting come morning!

I conducted many hunts out of these cabins. My niece Lynn Lovell, the daughter of my older brother, and I guided "soft adventure" (non-hunting) Potato Mountain trail rides out of it, and we lived there while ribboning the new trail up on Marmot Mountain. It was our "welcome home" cabin on returning from mountain goat hunts up Stikelan Creek.

## TAKING OVER THE MARION PLACE

We loved our little lane cabin along the Skinner Meadow access road, but since we had the Marion place back, we moved into the cabin Barry had set up for himself beside the Homathko River for the winter of 1978–79.

When we sold the ranch, I retained the Circle X brand, and we renamed the Marion place the Homathko Ranch. The 160 acres grew hay to feed our horses and provided winter pasture for them. The lane cabin remained a usable shelter for our family. Alex lived there for several years, as did our niece Lynn.

## MARMOT MOUNTAIN TRAIL

In the summer of 1969, Lynn helped me flag the trail to Marmot Mountain. Sometimes she was busy helping Alf on the sawmill, but she came when she could. I was busy as the family cook, but whenever a chainsawyer was available I went along to throw limbs and rocks off the cluttered trail. I'd take two saddle horses and a pack horse to carry the saw, gas and tools for the job.

I would tie the horses at the end of the cleared part, throw all the debris off the trail for two or three hundred yards, then hike back and bring the horses forward to have them and the gas and tools ready at hand. At the end of the day we'd ride home.

Eventually our trail was hacked through the forest to a well-used deer trail that angled up the open sidehill, which brought us out on top. Mission accomplished, though it took all of July and August. Then we had a family celebration on Marmot Mountain.

We packed two horses with our sleeping bags and enough food for two days and rode up the mountain in a little over three hours. This included stops all along the way to photograph the lovely alpine meadows on the mountain's flowered, undulating six-thousand- to seven-thousand-foot top. There is a spring-fed, six-metre pond we named Mirror Pond on top.

We found the most perfect campsite in a thick grove of balsam that gave shelter from the wind. The gentle ridge between two sloping, open meadows was rich with grass for our horses. Just below our campsite a clear, small spring bubbled out of the ground.

After we had lunch and laid in a supply of firewood for the night, we resaddled our horses for a rideabout to familiarize ourselves with the terrain. The horses had rolled and then fed for two hours, so they were ready to go. We staked the two pack horses, then rode up the grassy slope.

After a mile and a half we came upon a one-acre lake nestled in a break in the timbered ridge. It was fed by a huge snowbank deposited by winter winds on the leeward side of the ridge. This snowbank lasts all summer, providing water for deer, birds and mountain goats.

There were lots of deer tracks in the damp soil around the little lake, and a trickle of water ran out of the north end. How fortunate! All the other creeks on the mountain were in deep ravines. Our horses were thirsty, and we let them drink their fill after we filled up three one-gallon milk jugs to bring water back to camp.

Now riding above timberline we could view the north end of Chilko Lake and its huge, glacier-studded mountain range to the south. We could also see Tatlayoko Lake's mountains to the west.

The stunning view from the southside of Marmot Mountain.

What a sight! To the north was the Chilcotin Plateau. With binoculars we saw mule deer on neighbouring ridges coming out onto the grassy meadows to feed. That told us it was time to return to camp, so we turned our horses and rode down this central ridge back to camp, very satisfied with our exploring so far.

At camp we rigged a high pole to cache our food out of reach of predators. This high pole, well spaced between two clumps of trees, served us very well for many years.

The next job was to make a bedding space for each of us. The thickets were very enticing shelters, but very limby. Not to worry. Our chainsawyers carved cozy bedrooms in the thick foliage, making them spacey with headroom for standing. They even left some branches for hanging clothes on. The brush rubble was saved for a flash fuel source we could drop on the coals of a banked fire.

We enjoyed a sumptuous feast to honour the new trail and this marvellous mountain, and after washing the dishes, we hoisted our grub boxes up to the pole with ropes. We fell to sleep to the tinkling of the horse bells.

Up with the sun, we bucked up a bunch of firewood for our next trip and sawed campfire stools from a log. One sawyer went off to an adjacent thicket to build an outhouse. Good idea! We put a shovel on the list for our next trip to the mountain and added cushions for the stools as well.

We were all packed up, saddled and ready to leave by 10:00 a.m. On our way home, we groomed our new trail wherever it needed it. Over a late lunch and coffee at the mini-lodge, we told Alf and Leonard of this fabulous Marmot Mountain. We looked forward to taking guests up to enjoy it.

## FIRST GUESTS ON MARMOT, JULY 1980

Each winter I would advertise our Alpine Wilderness horseback tours and hunting trips. In the beginning, these trips only included tenting on Potato Mountain. Then we could advertise our Echo Lake cabin. Now we had Marmot.

In July 1980 we started reaping the rewards of our labours when four paying guests from Germany—two men and two women—booked a five-day wilderness trip on our previously inaccessible mountain.

They spent their first night in tents next to the Wilderness Lake mini-lodge to acclimate to the environment. They loved the sight of our favourite mountain mirrored on the smooth waters of Wilderness Lake the next morning. After a satisfying breakfast, we brought

Resting with a guest on Marmot Mountain.

the horses in from our newly fenced pasture to ride up Marmot Mountain.

We found our new trail just as we had left it. After two hours of riding, we followed the well-worn deer trail to the top, where we dismounted to water our horses at Mirror Pond. Then we re-mounted and continued to ride to the campsite we had chosen the previous year. We unsaddled all the horses so they could roll and graze.

Alex, my assistant, built the fire with wood we had stockpiled the year before. I handed out cups and took everyone to the little spring just below camp to have a drink of pure spring water. Then I dug a little reservoir with my cup to provide water for coffee.

We showed them the several "bedrooms" that our intrepid sawyers had cut in the thick alpine vegetation the previous summer. The men promptly put their sleeping gear down in two of them, but the women preferred a tent within view of the campfire.

Alex secured their tent to withstand any strong winds that might occur, but we rarely had gale-force winds in the summer months. The guests got busy with their cameras, photographing the luxuriously blooming meadows we had just ridden through. Just below the spring, the steady, gentle seepage irrigated the slope to produce a riot of colour: blue lupines, rose and pink Indian paintbrush, golden sunflowers and white daisies.

Then our guests walked fifty yards to the rim of the ridge to view and photograph the panorama from there. The green coniferous forest monopolized the view all the way down to the Tatlayoko Lake shoreline. The only exception was our postage-stamp clearing beside Wilderness Lake, which was the only habitation in sight. The rugged Coast Range rose from the western shoreline of Tatlayoko Lake, blotting out everything beyond that. After a light supper, everyone went to bed.

When breakfast was ready, a yodel brought our guests together, wide awake, to fill their plates with hotcakes, bacon and eggs. Our four pack boxes created handy storage shelves lying on their sides and stacked two high. They also provided two table surfaces.

We put cushions on the twelve-inch blocks of wood our sawyers

Our guests loved the ride to the top of Marmot Mountain, where they could photograph Potato Mountain, Chilko Lake and the Chilcotin Plateau.

had cut the previous summer, and we had a set of excellent stools. I washed the dishes, made lunches and then packed everything into the pack boxes, which Alex hoisted up out of reach on our high bar to protect our supplies from bears.

We staked the two pack horses using two forty-foot ropes tied to the forelock of one front foot, with the other end secured to a sturdy tree. Now we could ride up the bare grassy ridge glassing for deer in the deep, timbered valleys on either side.

We followed the rim eastward toward Chilko Lake and came out right above it. While standing on the narrow toe of a horseshoe at the top of the ridge, we happened to look down into the bowl's green slope and saw some very busy marmot activity there. On closer study with binoculars, we discovered they were running from den to den, wrestling and chasing each other. One big one, almost three feet tall, stood motionless. We took it to be the guardian. Should a bear, wolf or human appear, the sentinel would give a piercing whistle, whereupon each member of the colony would dive for cover. They entertained us for a while. Now we knew how Marmot Mountain got its name.

Going back to our grazing horses under Alex's watchful care, we remounted to ride further along Marmot Ridge, to the northeast, to peer down into a valley sloping up from the timber below. We dismounted to glass for wildlife. We were surprised to see about twenty mountain goats feeding on the lush green brush and grass there. We found comfortable places to sit and enjoy our lunch while watching the goats.

The goats also had a lookout posted. With their extraordinary clarity of vision, they soon spotted us and started moving toward a high pinnacle at the south end of a ridge. This was the highest point on Marmot. We watched as they lined out single file up onto the ridge, then followed the leader onto the peak. From there they spread out to circle the top and bed down.

The day was on the wane as we headed back to camp, well satisfied with what we had seen. Alex lowered the grub boxes from the high pole while I built the fire and put the coffee on. We unsaddled the horses, then staked and hobbled them.

Dinner was quick and easy. As the sun lowered, we walked to the western rim overlooking our trail home, looking for deer coming out to feed. We were rewarded when we spied a young two-point buck walking up the deer trail. Tatlayoko Valley was bathed in dusk.

We sat around the cheery campfire swapping stories until our guests sought their beds with flashlights. Alex switched the horses one more time while I tidied the camp and put a night log on the fire. Then we also tucked into our bedrolls to relax and enjoy the sweet, clean air and the tinkle of horse bells on our mountaintop.

After three nights on the mountain, our guests aired out their sleeping bags one last time while I made breakfast. Totally refreshed by our good night's sleep, we enjoyed the bright, sunny morning and the scent of the grass and flowers as we prepared to return to our mini-lodge base.

When we arrived at Wilderness Lake, Lynn had a nice lunch waiting for us. The horses, loose at last, bucked, kicked, rolled and trotted off for their unfettered freedom for a few days of well-earned rest.

We recounted our adventures to the satisfaction of Alf, Leonard and Lynn. Our guests sampled Wilderness Lake by going for a swim before changing into their travelling clothes for home—a five-hour drive to Williams Lake and a subsequent flight to Germany. They would be refreshed from their adventures in the wilds of British Columbia.

## NO MOOSE AROUND HERE

It was the second week of September and prime moose-hunting season in my region, depending on the weather. Not too hot, with cool, frosty nights. My party of two, Duke and Dan from California, had booked a seven-day moose hunt. When they arrived two days late, their one week of hunting time had shrunk to five days. We had previously booked a mountain-goat hunting party, and they would be arriving in six days.

Although I had planned to guide the two moose hunters myself, I now had to hire an assistant guide to hopefully make up for the two lost days. Leonard Billy, my assistant, was a fine moose hunter and an expert at butchering moose, so we thought we might make it work.

That first evening, just for luck, we took them over to nearby Wilderness Lake to check out the mineral lick that trickles out of the bank, soaking the muddy edges of the lake. There were plenty of deer tracks, but no fresh moose tracks.

The next morning at daylight, I took the two hunters over to the mineral lick again, while Leonard brought in our saddle horses and pack horses. We crept within one hundred yards of the lick, careful of our cover. There were two deer on the lick but no moose.

I decided to go further afield that day. While I made pocket lunches, Leonard saddled seven horses: four to ride and three to pack any meat if our hunt was successful. We mounted up and rode six miles to Moose Meadows.

Upon arrival I halted everyone to listen for moose grunting. Not hearing anything, I gave a grunt myself and waited at least fifteen minutes for an answer. Then we rode into the meadow to check for tracks. We saw a few tracks, but nothing fresh. We tied up the horses and split up our party, with Leonard and me each taking a hunter to check the surrounding area on foot. We would meet back at the creek in an hour.

There were a few tracks, but still no fresh ones. Since these meadows are so popular with the moose, we reasoned that it was still too early for the rut. The cow moose would still be secure with their spring calves deep in the jack pine jungle where a forest fire thirty years earlier had created a thick growth of young trees. The young animals would be safe from predators in this fire-killed nursery until they developed longer legs and more muscular bodies.

This moose pasture would have to wait until the cows came into their annual breeding season, another week maybe, depending on the weather. We rode back, getting home before dark.

The next day I rousted everyone early to step up lively. We would pack up onto Marmot Mountain to take advantage of the new trail we had ribboned and cut the previous year. There was a brushy moose pasture on the north end of the mountain, about halfway up. We could walk quietly along the new trail and peek through the needled fringe of trees to scan the moose meadows.

We prepared ourselves for camping out at Mirror Pond and took three extra horses to pack out a moose if we got one.

I was delighted to ride up my new Marmot Mountain trail. After three hours we topped out at our campsite and unsaddled and unpacked our gear. I built a cooking fire for supper and took a pail over to Mirror Pond for water to make coffee.

Leonard watered and staked three horses and hobbled the rest to graze the three acres of grassy open meadow. With our tents up, we were fortified by a good lunch and we all needed a nap. We were at six thousand feet elevation by now.

After our rest we hiked partway down the trail to look for moose tracks but saw no sign on our quick check. I noticed sour faces on both Leonard and Duke when we returned to camp. I had explained to the hunters that the moose were higher up on the cooler north side of the mountain and that we were going to check that out the next day thoroughly.

"Hrumph, no moose around here," said Leonard, as he went out to restake the horses.

I hadn't expected such blatant insubordination from my assistant guide. Then I realized he was mostly empathizing with Duke, who persisted in being glum. I guessed Duke was a man of importance in his own element, which probably didn't include women in charge. The other hunter, Dan, was the silent partner and seemed agreeable to my suggestions.

After a quick supper we all sought our separate beds. I was used to guests who liked to sit around the campfire after supper and exchange hunting stories and absorb the sights and sounds of camp life. I banked the fire to keep curious wildlife out of our camp and turned in, hoping for an improvement in Duke's attitude in the morning.

With daylight coming on, I got up to build the fire for cooking and fetched some water for coffee. Leonard, always an early riser, staked the horses that had been hobbled for the night and put hobbles on the horses that had been staked. Then he replenished the pile of firewood to make a quick fire later and a pile for overnight.

I cooked a hearty breakfast and made sandwiches for lunch. As soon as the men were through eating, I washed up the dishes and stored them in the pack boxes to be hoisted to our high bar.

Leonard saddled the four horses we were going to use that day and staked the other horses on fresh pasture in the meadow. I handed the men their lunches to put in their saddlebags, drowned the campfire with water and mounted my horse to lead the group to the north-end moose pasture.

When we arrived and staked our horses, I motioned everyone in close so I could quietly explain the plan.

"Leonard, you and Duke will walk slowly and quietly down the new side trail looking out toward the middle of the meadows. You may hear a grunt, so listen often. Dan and I will work our way along through the bushy willows. If either party spooks a bull, he will likely run into the other party. Okay?"

Before we left, Duke came over to me complaining that Leonard told him he had never hunted here before and didn't know the country. I pointed out they had a well-used game trail to follow. "Just move downhill on the trail that hugs the pine-tree line all the way. I'll keep 350 yards between us, and we'll meet you back at the horses in four hours."

Both Leonard and Duke had sour faces as they prepared to head down the trail. I heard Leonard repeat his gripe from the day before. "Hrrmph ... No moose around here!"

"We don't know that," I patiently replied. "The forage looks good. Just the trail is new. Watch for tracks."

Dan and I made our way into the willows. It was about eleven o'clock and I took the lead, skirting the band of willows and short chunky pines bordering the natural meadows. Halfway down I stepped on a wet patch of grass. There were moose tracks beside it and a strong scent of moose. The moisture was moose urine. A cow moose had urinated there that morning, and a bull had validated her sign. His big hoofprints were clearly imprinted on the wet patch and trodden-down grass.

I pointed this out to my hunter, pressing my right index finger across my lips. We needed to breach this band of willow clumps and short ridges of pine for a view of the open meadow. And we needed to do it silently, which I thoroughly impressed on Dan by hand signals.

I slowly crossed the willow/pine fringe, searching for a trail into the open meadow. My all-woollen clothing slid silently though the bordering branches and Dan followed suit.

We came to a gap in the pines and I peeked out from behind a few branches. A bull moose was facing me, looking and listening. He was in the open meadow with only knee-high willows between us. I sat still and silent, waiting for Dan to catch up. When he was right behind me I pointed to the meadow with my finger over my mouth. He was astonished. The bull was one hundred yards off, looking directly at us, guided by his big ears that were picking up the slightest sounds. He could have escaped but curiosity overtook him.

Dan was now in shooting position, with one knee on the ridge and one knee supporting the rifle. He had quietly slid a shell into the chamber. I tugged at his jacket to bring his ear close for my whispered instructions. "Your best shot is his chest, but his big nose is covering it. You have to wait until he turns his head, then shoot dead centre in his chest."

We breathed softly and quietly. With no sound coming from our brushy ridge, the bull glanced to the right to check on his cow.

"Now!" I whispered.

Dan squeezed the trigger and ka-boom! The bull disappeared behind the knee-high grass and willows. We could see the brush quivering.

"Reload!" I commanded. "Be ready if he gets up."

We both stood, awaiting what might happen next, and we were not prepared for it. A bellow to wake the dead came from Duke, who was attacking the thick willow patch to our right, waving his rifle and fighting the head-high willows. Suddenly he yelled, "He's getting away! Shoot him! Shoot him!"

We could see the cow running by, and Leonard put his hand on Duke's rifle. "It's a cow," he said.

Dan and I silently watched this charade while keeping an eye on the short willows where Dan's bull had fallen. He was dead for sure by now.

When Duke and Leonard got to Dan's bull before we did, Duke fired his rifle into the head of the dead animal.

Leonard's face was all smiles as he opened the carcass of Dan's bull to remove its innards and drain the blood. I didn't say a word about his earlier statement: "No moose around here." Instead I said I'd go get their lunches before heading back to the camp for the pack horses a mile away. By the time I got back an hour later, Leonard had the moose cleaned and quartered.

A few drops of rain indicated a storm was brewing as the men hastily loaded the moose quarters onto the two pack horses. We lashed the antlers on top of the front quarters and were off, leaving the skull and forelegs for the coyotes.

At camp we off-loaded the moose carcass onto a clean tarp, then covered the mound with another clean tarp held down with boulders. By that time it was raining hard and we didn't anticipate predators.

Boiling water over a campfire for a nice warm cup of coffee. Building a fire is a critical backcountry skill.

I built a fire from the dry wood I had kept in my roomy tent and soon had hot water boiling for coffee. Hot vegetable soup warmed us as Leonard staked and hobbled the horses. We hurried into our tents for shelter, taking our hot bowls of soup with us.

In spite of the rain, we all went to bed relaxed and happy. Dan was very satisfied with his first moose hunt.

The morning dawned clear and sunny and we enjoyed a relaxing breakfast with moose liver fried with bacon and campfire toast. I cleaned the camp and Leonard cut firewood to supply our next use of this camp. Then he caught and saddled all seven horses for our journey home.

At Wilderness Lake, my family congratulated Dan on getting his first moose. After lunch Leonard offered to take Duke up to Tanya Lake, just in case, but they had no luck.

As the hunters left the next morning, this whole incident reminded me of how difficult it can be for a woman in a male-dominated profession. Any woman who wants to be a guide outfitter has to realize she has got to deal with criticism from men who think they know better.

## CURSING AND SWEARING

I've had several men as guests who have wives and families they cherish back home. But out on the trail they easily forget that I am a woman. Sometimes they need a reminder.

One year I had a hunting party at the south end of Tatlayoko Lake. We had this little trapper's cabin we could use. I cooked and they ate their meals in there, but the hunters slept outside in tents because the cabin was so small.

As soon as I was up making breakfast they'd come in. It was September and we were right on the shoreline of the lake—a really nice place. These guys started telling these smutty stories while I was trying to make breakfast.

Soon I told them, "Hold it, I don't enjoy these stories you're telling that put women down." Horrible stuff. I said, "Do you think you could stop telling them in my presence? I'll give you plenty of time to tell your stories. I'm going to leave the room, and when you're done, you whistle and I'll come back and make the breakfast."

That's how I got around that.

"Okay, Gerry," they said and laughed.

I went out and puttered around in the yard and they told their stories, then they went to the door and said, "All done!" And I came in and finished making breakfast.


## NOVEMBER HORSE ROUNDUP

By the end of the fall, our horse herd certainly deserved time off. They had worked steadily and faithfully all summer carrying our guests up onto Potato Mountain or Marmot Mountain to experience the alpine flower fields, trout streams and breathtaking scenery.

Then in September they had to scramble up steeper and narrower trails in moose and mountain-goat country, carrying hunting guests and all the necessary camping paraphernalia. Then they had to pack heavy quarters of moose from hidden swamp meadows for miles, before being unburdened at Wilderness Lake cabin where our truck was parked.

In the summer our horses grazed in some beautiful country with top grade clover for feed. My horse Butternut sneaks a little snack while Griz keeps watch.

With hunting season over, the horse herd was running free on our fall range past Wilderness Lake, enjoying themselves before coming home to the valley for the winter. There they would be fed top-quality hay every day, both wild and tame varieties of clover, timothy and alfalfa.

When the first serious snowfall came in late November, Alf and I decided it was time to bring the horse herd back to the Marion place so we could feed them. Because their range at Wilderness Lake was at 4,500 feet elevation, there would be more snow there than in the 2,700-foot Tatlayoko Valley. They could easily be snowed in.

We loaded six fifty-pound bales of hay into our pickup box, along with my sleeping bag, saddle, bridle, several halters and enough food for myself for four days, and drove the twenty miles to our cabin at Wilderness Lake.

Alf returned to the Marion place for evening chores while I stayed comfortably in the cabin to await the arrival of the horses, which often happened at night when they wanted the salt. I would hear the bells, hurry out to shut the gate on them, then break and scatter the six bales so the herd of twenty-six horses would have equal rations. Then in the morning, I would saddle the leader, and leading a couple of bunch quitters, we would all start the long trek for home.

I had plenty of firewood and Alf had chopped a waterhole in the lake ice in front of the cabin. With a shelf of good books to choose from, and a gas lantern to read by, I settled in for my enforced holiday to enjoy my time alone, with only myself to cook for and cater to.

The snow was about twenty inches deep at the cabin and was likely deeper further up the valley and up the mountainside, where the horses were pawing for dry grass. Those horses knew the routine. They would be coming in soon.

There was no sound of bells that first night. I couldn't be that lucky. But they could arrive anytime during the day. I found it difficult to keep busy. It got dark early in the day that time of year and I would have to leave early in the day if I needed to go hunt them. *I'll just give them a little more time*, I thought. *The older horses will decide to come on in, and the younger ones will follow.* That's what I hoped.

When I went to bed the second night I couldn't sleep. I kept lying there hoping to hear the horse bells. Then I heard something that made my blood run cold. A pack of wolves came through in the night, travelling on the lake ice and howling their mournful yo-delling—a blood-chilling symphony. I awoke with a start, worried anew about our horses.

I went out onto the doorstep, expecting to see the wolf pack, but there was no moon or stars and the sky was overcast. But the echoes of the howling rebounding off the surrounding hills was an experience I'll never forget.

My sleep was fitful the rest of that night, even though the wolves had moved on and silence had been restored. When I did fall asleep, I dreamed all about wolves, dreams spawned from the true stories I had been told by rugged guide outfitters and trappers. A pack of wolves attacked a young, healthy cow moose, running alongside her on a frozen lake and ripping her flank open. The six-month-old developing fetus fell out, and the wolves fought over it and devoured it. The mother, with her hind legs entangled in her intestines, stood off awaiting the inevitable.

In another story, a Chilcotin rancher had his herd of horses rustling on a swamp meadow, pawing the snow away to eat the hay. Three of his horses were killed by a pair of wolves who hamstrung them, ripping the main tendon on the back of their hind legs to bring them down. The wolves had a feeding frenzy.

Needless to say my mind was made up. I would go immediately to find our horse herd and bring them home. At first light I hastily made a pocket lunch, banked the heater fire and dressed myself in my all-woollen army-issue clothes, which would keep me warm even if they got wet. Then I pulled my gumboots over my woollen socks.

I draped my bridle and halters around my neck and over one shoulder, stowed a small bag of oats in my pocket and set off up the valley looking for signs of the horses. I wanted to take my 30-30, but it was too much to carry. Ideally I needed a pistol.

It was slow going through the knee-deep snow, but I knew where to look. I had gone out on foot all summer to bring in certain horses. They knew my call and would come for the treat of oats they knew I always carried.

The sky showed a sullen overcast. One more snowfall would make it impossible to walk and would cover their tracks as well.

I wished I had kept my saddle horse in. Riding him would have made it so much easier, as he would have scented the herd and gone straight to them. But he would have been unhappy all by himself in the corral at the cabin. In later years we have gone out on a snowmobile to bring in the horses, but we weren't equipped with them yet.

The fir branches were heavy with snow and I had to stay back from the smaller trees to avoid getting soaked. It was easier to walk under the bigger, older firs because the snow was not so deep, having been caught by the bigger, stronger limbs. This is why mule deer can winter well in a fir-timbered forest. A heavy snow will break the brittle branches off, providing the mule deer with food to sustain them until conditions improve.

I took time out for half a sandwich. Now slogging uphill, I was hoping to find their tracks on the mountainside. I saw no fresh tracks in the first two miles and stopped often to catch my breath and listen for horse bells. The snow on the tree limbs muffled the sound as I zigzagged uphill to about the 4,800-foot level and started hiking in a large circle. Within twenty minutes I came upon day-old horse tracks. Still no sound of bells, but I knew I had them within my half-circle on the south side of Marmot Mountain.

After maintaining a level course at 4,500 feet for a half mile, I dropped downhill to begin closing my circle and found them within it. They were pawing the fluffy snow for the bunch grass underneath. Once the snow crusts, the horses can starve. The icy crust can cut their ankles, and then they stop pawing.

They stood just looking at me, too tired from pawing snow to make the effort of coming for grain. I walked right up to the lead horse, talking to all of them as I always do: "Hey boys, why didn't you all come in? There's hay waiting for you, you know that! And no work for six months!"

They didn't move to gather around me like they usually do. This alone told me a lot. Even though they looked good, well furred and fleshed out, the constant pawing in that deep snow was draining their energies. But they were all present, thankfully.

I soon had a couple haltered and I tail-tied one to the other. Then I hopped up on the leader's bare back, and with a cheery "Come on, boys!" we led off. All the others began to follow.

Within the hour they were all in the corral. I took off the bridle and halters, then spread the baled hay all over the roomy corral so everyone would get enough. They could spend the night there and we'd get an early start in the morning for the Marion place. That night their bells were music to my grateful ears.

My cabin was still warm and cozy. I stoked up the fire, heated some food, lit the gas lantern and, with my book for entertainment, settled in for an enjoyable evening. We would all be home tomorrow.

# BUILDING THE BIG LODGE

When our son Kevan married his wife, Lynn, they moved to Kamloops so he could develop a trade. He became a very good welder but detested the conditions of the job like the bad fumes and very poor ventilation. When he got laid off for the winter in the fall of 1982, he drew up plans for a twenty-six-room lodge. In the spring he brought the blueprints to Alf and me to consider.

Kevan really surprised us. We were only planning to build a small log cabin on our Lot 230, about a mile from Wilderness Lake. Then he said, "Mother, you always wanted a lodge for your guests and hunters. So here are the blueprints. See if you like them and we'll start on it because I'm not working at the moment."

He had a whole booklet of detailed drawings including one of a staircase, starting wide at the bottom and tapering narrow at the top. We liked it.

## FIXING UP THE A-FRAME

We didn't have any place to sleep close to where we wanted to build the lodge, and our mini-lodge on Wilderness Lake was a mile away. Barry had hauled a little cabin to the lease for Alf and Leonard Billy to stay in while they were clearing the land. He had also hauled in the shell of an A-frame I purchased for one hundred dollars from the manager of the Tatlayoko Mill when it burned down, but we hadn't done anything with it yet.

Barry hauled in this cabin for the men to sleep in while they cleared the land.

We put the A-frame right beside the creek so we'd have water for cooking, and Kevan got right into fixing it up. He built a loft for sleeping and put in a circular staircase that went round and round this great big log. Then he boxed it in. The whole upstairs was bunk beds for workers building the lodge.

Kevan brought in a crew of men he recruited from the bars in Kamloops. They would work for two weeks, then when Kevan would go home to see his family, he'd take them all with him. After a few days he'd return with his crew.

We got this German lady, Anna Schlingermann, to be our cook. Her husband had died and she had come to Canada with her sixteen-year-old daughter. She was ready to marry somebody else and wanted to find a boyfriend for her daughter.

It worked out very well for us because we had them there all summer. But this young girl was a bit of a distraction to the work-ers. She would lie on the porch steps wearing her shorts or some-thing scanty, and the men would have to step over her to go to work. She eventually ended up marrying a young rancher and they have a beautiful home next to her mother, so it all worked out.

This A-frame came from the Lignum mill. It eventually became our staff quarters for the lodge.

Anna was a marvellous cook and a very cheerful lady. We moved her into the A-frame as soon as Kevan got it liveable. He kept working on the A-frame because we couldn't do anything on the lodge until the ground dried out. So that was our first cabin on the property.

Once the lodge was finished, we continued using the A-frame as a staff quarters. Anyone who worked at the lodge lived there. It's been really handy. For one hundred dollars I really got my money's worth.

## ALPINE WILDERNESS LODGE

The Alpine Wilderness Lodge, as we named it, was Kevan's inspiration. It was he who spearheaded building it. We began construction in the summer of 1983, but we couldn't use our big-wheeled loader or other heavy equipment until July because the ground was so soft. There's so much snow in there, the machinery would just bog down.

The lodge took a lot of effort. We were building on it from July

Laying the foundation in the heat of the summer was back-breaking work.

right to snow time for several years. I've got many pictures because I kept taking them every day as the lodge was being built. When I took lunches over, I'd ask them what part of the lodge they were doing that day and then I'd go take pictures.

The first year, all we got done was the back wall and one end wall of upright timbers and some flooring.

We used our own timbers that Alf milled from logs taken off the lease. There was a great deal of chinking to do, and Leonard and Alf worked together using a caulking gun to fill the cracks. Leonard applied the caulking while Alf smoothed it with a knife. No fuss, no mess, just a very tidy job.

We wanted to get as much value out of the logs taken off the lease as we could. There was a good market for railway ties, so Alf cut ties along with timbers for the house. When the big trucks hauling cement and other building materials arrived from town, Alf sent loads of ties out as a backhaul to pay for the trucking.

During the summer and fall of 1984, we got the rest of the walls up and put the roof on, but not before we had a close call

We used timber from Alf's lease land and milled it on the property.

Below: Alf's sawmill at Wilderness Lake.

The crew laying the notching timbers.

It took three years to finish the lodge so we could move in, but it the end we had a beautiful spacious new home.

with the weather. In September, Kevan had taken his work crew to Kamloops for a few days when we got four inches of snow. The roof wasn't on and the flooring had all been freshly varnished and oiled.

When Kevan left it was a beautiful sunny day, but by afternoon a big thunderstorm had rolled in. By evening it started snowing and it snowed all night. The snow filled the whole upstairs of the building. Everybody was gone except my two hunters from Europe and my girlfriend from Riske Creek and her eighty-four-year-old hunter friend.

I had to organize getting the snow out of there before it ruined the floor. The snow was already melting when I started clearing it out. We only had one snow shovel and the lodge was huge, so I got pieces of plywood and we used them to push the snow. Somebody cleaned the snow out of the bedrooms, and someone else shoved it down the long hallways and dumped it out the big windows in the front.

When Kevan got back he was thankful we had protected the floor. He didn't waste any time getting the roof on before any more snow started to fly. Once the roof was on, we could work on the inside of the building late into the fall, as long as we could get the building materials to the site.

It took three years before we could move into the lodge. It wasn't even finished when we accommodated our first guests in 1985. We continued working on the inside finishing work, plumbing and bathrooms. Every guest room had its own bathroom—a landmark in Chilcotin history. Kevan welded up the big furnace right in the lodge. It's gigantic. The part downstairs is a huge three-sided thing as tall as me. There's another one just like it upstairs, but we never have to light it because the bottom warms the upstairs just fine.

One of the workers Kevan recruited from the Kamloops beer parlour built all our furniture. He was an alcoholic and his wife had left him because of his drinking, but he didn't drink when he was working with us. When he went home on weekends he'd get roaring drunk. He was a great carpenter and he built all of our chairs, settees and coffee tables. I directed him to put a little glamour into his work because the wood was so plain. I got a piece of paper and measured it to fit the top of the chairs and drew a scroll. He used the scroll design on all the furniture.

## FUN-FILLED SUMMERS

Those summers we spent building the lodge were fun-filled and exciting times. Kevan's wife, Lynn, and their two children, Thea and Ryan, spent the summers with us. Barry's daughters, Tanya and Brenda, lived with Alf and me for five years at that time as well.

Brenda, at nine, would go out alone to the horse pasture and climb onto each of our nine loose horses, bareback, with no halter or bridle. Then she would come in and proudly tell me what she had done. It could have been a tribute to our gentle horses, or that she was becoming a horse whisperer. The grandkids all became good riders.

Alf and me standing in front of the A-frame cabin that I purchased for $100. Kevan fixed it up for the work crew to stay in while we built the main lodge.

All four grandchildren's birthdays are during the winter whereas mine is mid-July, so I staged a summertime birthday for all of us. We had treasure hunts outdoors, played hide-and-seek and went rafting and swimming on Wilderness Lake. We would dive into the warm twelve-foot depths from the raft. Then we'd go back to the lodge kitchen, where each birthday child made and decorated her or his own cake. I coached the two youngest with the ingredients, quantities, mixing and baking, and they loved it. But when it came to decorating, I put out the icing sugar mix and they spread it on themselves. The bottled food colouring turned the icing into pretty flowers, hearts and rainbows drawn by the three girls. One year Ryan, the only boy, built a dark mountain exploding in a brilliant red volcano and a red river of lava running across the cake.

Celebrating my birthday along with the grandkids for a few years was the best birthday a grandmother could have had.

By 1985 we had our lives organized. In May we had spring bear hunting at the lodge. In July and August we conducted trail rides from the lodge or mini-lodge. In late August we put up hay on Lot 230 and at the Marion place. September 1 was the beginning of mountain-goat hunting, followed by moose and mule-deer hunting right to December 1. Then we shut everything down and moved ourselves, the kids and the horses, along with their baled hay, up to the Marion place for winter.

At first Tanya and Brenda were too young for school, and then they started attending classes down the road at Tatlayoko School. In May of 1988, Alex and his girlfriend, Connie, got married at the lodge, and they lived with us the following winter. Alf and Alex built a six-by-twenty-foot extra room onto the mill shack that Alf and I occupied at the Marion place. They built it in two days out of milled timbers from Alf's mill to provide extra space for Alex and Connie.

Alex bought a new log cabin shell, moved it onto the Marion place and finished it with our carpenter friend, Carl Buchholtz. We all lived snugly together that winter, feeding our herd of gentle dude horses and waiting for spring so we could go back to Lot 230 and Wilderness Lodge.

## KEVAN PULLS OUT OF ALPINE WILDERNESS LODGE

Eventually Kevan and Lynn just wanted to go and have a life of their own. When we got done building the lodge they didn't want to stay there, and Kevan wanted a guiding area of his own. We gave him money for his help in building the lodge, and he bought Dave

In 1985 the lodge was finally ready for our first guests.

Wilson's old guiding territory north of Tatla Lake. He ran it for a year, then found a territory he liked better in the South Chilcotin.

He met an old couple in Kamloops who wanted to retire and bought their territory on Gunn Creek in the Bridge River country, but he's got these mountains that are all straight up and down. Not like mine, where you can ride everywhere.

Alex and Kevan worked together really well on the lodge, but both of them agreed they wished they'd never started it because it was killing them off. By the time it was done, they were wearing out from all the hard work. The ten-thousand-square-foot all-log lodge built from logs harvested and milled onsite is a testament to the hard work, vision and dedication of Kevan, Alex and Alf. It truly is a four-season wilderness tourism legacy.

## THE WINDS OF TATLAYOKO

The coastal gale-force winds that come off the Pacific Ocean up Bute Inlet and roar through the Homathko River canyon and terrorize the settlers north of Tatlayoko Lake are legendary. They have blown down big fir trees and scattered whole sections of log fence that

Serene Tatlayoko Lake is a force to be reckoned with when the wind picks up.

took two men days to build working together and then to rebuild.

Fifteen-mile-long Tatlayoko Lake, right in its path, becomes churned to a froth. No one wishes to be caught out on the lake when that big wind blows.

One March, a neighbour was awakened during the night by the sounds of his roof being ripped off, plank by plank. He ran outside and the wind caught him as well. He fell on the ice sheet that was his yard and was blown across it along with the planks from his roof. He was fortunate not to be hit by another roof plank, which narrowly missed him. He ended up selling that exposed property and moved to a place more sheltered.

One day I'll never forget, my son Marty and I were guiding a mule-deer hunter named Jack on Potato Mountain. It was October and we were riding up to scan the high alpine at six or seven thousand feet for a big buck to stalk.

At that altitude, there are only very scattered patches of short scrub evergreens. The bucks would creep into them to hide during the day, or they would move from patch to patch.

It was a lovely day, blue sky and a light southerly breeze. We had no luck there, and the breeze started to increase to gusts of wind. The bucks, always alert to weather changes, must have moved downhill into the timber ahead of the wind.

We moved down, still searching. The wind increased and storm clouds appeared on the horizon, blotting out the view of the jagged Coast Range peaks across the valley. It was time to leave the mountain for the shelter of our lodge.

As we followed the horse trail into the dense jack pine timber, the wind increased. When we began hearing trees crashing in the forest, we became wary of the tall pines lining both sides of the trail. We would stop a full tree's length away from the forest so no tree could clobber us during a violent gust. When the gust subsided, we rode on through.

We had four miles of this narrow forested trail to ride before reaching our cleared pasture land and hayfield at the lodge. Even our saddle and pack horses were jumpy when they heard the trees breaking off and crashing in the forest.

Finally the end was in sight. Six tall pines stood at the confluence of the meadow and the trail. They were bending violently in a gust. I called a halt to wait for the calmer period between gusts.

When it came, we urged our horses into high gear and dashed through onto the meadow. The lodge was now in sight with just another half mile of level, treeless trail to go. We could relax at last.

The next day dawned calm and cloudless, and our hunter, Jack, was game for adventure. We knew we would have to clear our mountain trail of windfalls before we could use it: seven miles through timber standing broadside to the gale.

We left after breakfast and expected to be home for lunch. We anticipated that maybe a dozen trees needed bucking, so we only took one chainsaw. Those last six pines at the end of the trail were all down across the trail! We bucked them up for future firewood and went on, cutting and clearing the four miles to the steeper climb up the south end of Potato Mountain.

By this time we were out of gas and had no choice but to go back to the lodge for a very late lunch. We decided to finish cutting the trail the next day when we would be going back up to finish the hunt.

Jack was enjoying the novelty of "wrastling with nature," as he called it, and overnighting at the lodge and having a shower wasn't expected until the hunt ended. Now he was refreshed and rested for the remainder of his trip. We rode back up the next day and ate our lunches and went hunting. We estimated 105 trees had closed the trail.

The deer started moving by 4 p.m., restless after their enforced bushing-up from the raging storm. Strange how they knew in advance. We located a buck, tied up our horses and stalked it on foot. "Fair Chase" Jack made a clean shot from 250 yards, and we congratulated him. We cleaned it and packed it to our mountain cabin to hang and cool out overnight. Next morning, rested and successful, we packed everything and rode home to the lodge and his truck. Jack thanked us, paid us and left happy.

# FROM PRAIRIE GIRL TO MOUNTAIN WOMAN

I am no longer able to climb the mountains and head out down the trail on horseback like I used to. Many vivid memories of my guiding and outfitting days entertain me, but those days are not completely behind me.

When Alex, who is now our family guide outfitter, comes home from a hunt or taking backcountry adventurers over the trails, I revel in the stories that he and his clients tell.

Soft-adventure guests and seasonal hunters come from all over the world to sample our pure wilderness and our brand of hospitality. Most of our European guests speak enough English that we can converse with pleasure.

Seventy-five years ago, I came to British Columbia from the prairies of Alberta searching for mountains. I was so blessed to find my home in Tatlayoko Valley, nestled in the wilderness surrounded by the high peaks of the Pacific Coast Range. Not only did I find the mountains, I found a whole new way of life and a way of sharing this special place with people from around the world.

## ALF'S LEGACY

Because Alf was one of two bulldozer operators who built the historic road through the Coast Mountains from Anahim Lake to the

Enjoying the Sunshine in the garden at the Wilderness Lodge.

Bella Coola Valley during the summers of 1952 and 1953, we managed to get a mountain range named after him.

It was impossible to do this while Alf was still alive. But when he passed away in August 2006 at eighty-three, we were honoured to have the Alf Bracewell Mountain Range officially designated south of Potato Mountain. There are many unnamed peaks in the vast Coast Mountains, but we started calling the mountain that reflects in Wilderness Lake Alf Bracewell Mountain once Alf started clearing Lot 230 and we built our mini-lodge next to the lake.

Alf and I were married for fifty-two years. We raised our family to love and respect the outdoors.

Alf and I were married for fifty-two and a half years and lived a happy and rewarding life together, fulfilling our dreams. From our four sons, Marty, Barry, Kevan and Alex, we have nine grandchildren and two great-grandchildren.

Barry had Tanya and Brenda with his first wife, Caroline; then Mike and Patricia with his second wife, Tess. Kevan and Lynn had Thea and Ryan, and Alex and Connie had Bobidaia, Aaron and Anna. Our granddaughter Tanya gave us two great-grandchildren, Morgyn and Liam.

My grandchildren are all good with horses, both riding and training them. I bought many of them horses before they were school age. Alex's daughter Bobidaia is an exceptional horse trainer and rider. In 2011 she won the famed Mountain Race at the Williams Lake Stampede, and she was up against all male riders. It is gratifying to have my granddaughter carry on the tradition of a woman excelling in an activity typically dominated by men. I like to think I've inspired all my grandchildren to push themselves to achieve their dreams.

Riding on Potato Mountain with Tatlayoko Lake below and peaks of the Niut and Coast Range beyond.

Above: Heading to the Potato Mountain alpine.

Below: I trained my horses to sit still when I was loading game onto their backs.

Above: Field dressing a freshly killed bear.

Below: Weather was no excuse when there was a job to be done.